T0163100

JOSH GIBSON

William Brashler is also the author of *The Bingo Long Traveling All-Stars and Motor Kings*, the highly regarded novel of a touring black baseball team in the pre—Jackie Robinson era, as well as two other novels, *City Dogs* and *Traders*, and *The Don: The Life and Death of Sam Giancana*. He lives and writes in Chicago.

JOSH GIBSON

A Life in the Negro Leagues

William Brashler

Ivan R. Dee

Chicago

JOSH GIBSON. Copyright © 1978, 2000 by William Brashler. This book was first published in 1978 and is here reprinted by arrangement with the author. First Ivan R. Dee paperback edition published 2000. For information, address: Ivan R. Dee, Publisher, 1332 North Halsted Street, Chicago 60622. Manufactured in the United States of America and printed on acid-free paper.

Library of Congress Cataloging-in-Publication Data:
Brashler, William.
    Josh Gibson : a life in the Negro leagues / William Brashler.
        p.   cm.
    Originally published: New York : Harper & Row, c1978.
    Includes index.
    ISBN 1-56663-295-1 (alk. paper)
    1. Gibson, Josh, 1911–1947.   2. Baseball players—United States—Biography.
3. Negro leagues.   I. Title.
GV865.G53 B7 2000
796.357'092—dc21
    [B]   99-057926

Contents

A section of photographs follows page 76.

Acknowledgments

One cannot write a novel about the Negro baseball leagues as I did without one day wanting to go back and delve into that rich era of history. Little was ever recorded concerning the Negro game, however, and research materials are sparse. All baseball historians owe a debt to Robert Peterson for his *Only the Ball Was White*, the first comprehensive look at the Negro era and a book which stands as an authoritative, thorough guide to the black leagues. Peterson's book pointed me in the right directions, and I shall always prize it.

Like Peterson, I went to black newspapers for the day-to-day information on the black leagues, as sketchily as it may have been reported. I am grateful to the Chicago Historical Society for access to its microfilm of the Chicago *Defender*, and to the Carnegie Library in Pittsburgh with its holdings of the Pittsburgh *Courier*.

My primary source of material and insight, however, came from the people who somehow participated in the era. They shared with me their time and their glowing memories, and I am indebted to them.

They include:

Josh Gibson's fine teammates and their wives: James "Cool Papa" Bell and his wife, Clarabelle; Jimmie Crutchfield and his wife, Julia; Vic Harris and his wife, Dorothy; Ted Page; and Sam Streeter.

Jack Marshall; David Malarcher; and Normal "Tweed" Webb.

David McCormick, for his insights and access to his fine

library of taped interviews with such former Negro league players as Judy Johnson, Buck Leonard, Johnny Hayes, Alex Radcliffe, Satchel Paige, and Roy Campanella.

William Price Fox, for the germ of the idea way back when, and sessions with his grand tapes of Satchel Paige.

Helen Bankhead; Ethel Posey Maddox; Mrs. Wendell Smith; and Jim Brosnan.

Introduction:
Notes on a Low Line Drive

He died in the early morning hours of January 20, 1947. Almost seven months later, I was born. There is little else to connect me and my life to that of Josh Gibson. I never sat behind backstops watching him crack towering drives out of small-town ballparks, nor did I listen to his exploits on the radio or watch them on black-and-white television, nor did I collect his baseball card, or, for that matter, ever see his face on a baseball card.

Still, there is a thread of a relationship between us, between Josh and the white and black kids I grew up with who were baseball players and baseball fans. And I'll claim that link, treasure it, even visualize what the man must have looked like, his stride, the electric moment when his bat met the ball and it exploded and soared out of sight, leaving only the frozen image of its amazing trajectory. And anybody who has seen such a phenomenon, by Josh or someone else, won't begrudge me the memory or the secret, covetous feeling that that home run was my home run.

Ten years after the night of Josh Gibson's death, I saw my first major league baseball game, an event for people of my generation and many before it that was a certain kind of ritual. In Grand Rapids, Michigan, where I grew up, it meant a trip to Detroit and what was then called Briggs Stadium, home of the Detroit Tigers. It wasn't a family affair but a fruit of Little League. My team was the Eberhard Giants, sponsored by the Eberhard grocery stores, and for five scintillating summers I wore its green and gray uniform.

There was no little amount of excitement that morning of my first train ride across the state to Detroit in the summer of 1957. With 110 other Little Leaguers, I marched out of Detroit's train terminal over to Michigan and Trumball streets and Briggs Stadium. Even though the place was scarcely an architectural landmark, or even a particularly attractive ballpark, I was awed. I had never seen anything as big and as green in my life. I sat down in a bleacher seat behind the left fielder and continued to marvel. There was little else to do, for the seats were so poor, and so far away from the action, that what was going on in the infield barely resembled the game of baseball that I played.

The only thing real was one of the players on the opposing team, the Boston Red Sox, a puckish, toothy guy named Jimmy Piersall. Throughout his team's pre-game workout, Piersall turned and mugged at us, sticking out his tongue, hooting, throwing baseballs at the screen, and generally astounding us all. We knew little of his mental difficulties or what particular devils were hounding him that day. We knew only that we liked anyone who paid attention to us, and that Detroit's left fielder, a colorless left-hander named Charlie Maxwell, ignored us completely.

The game began, progressed, and amazed none of us. Detroit and the Red Sox were not very impressive clubs, even to Little Leaguers. We were scarcely aware that all the faces on each team were white, that these two clubs in 1957 had yet to put a black player on its parent roster. It was ten years after Jackie Robinson, yet neither team was to get a bona fide black star for another three years. (Boston was to be the last club to include a black, Pumpsie Green in 1959, an item of baseball trivia instead of a landmark.)

But the Red Sox did have Ted Williams, a genuine superstar, and though he paid no attention to us when he came into left field, he did take occasion to slam a line drive into the right-field seats for a home run. It wasn't a towering, Williamsonian blast that shot into the heavens and plopped down onto the stadium roof, but a low screamer that made it past Al Kaline's glove in right field, then over the short screen behind him, all in a second, a drive that if you looked down to shell a peanut, you would have missed.

It was Williams nine years later, however, upon his induction into the Hall of Fame, who said a few words that awakened baseball fans all over.

"The other day, Willie Mays hit his 522nd home run," Williams said at the microphone in Cooperstown, New York. "He's gone past me, and he's pushing, and I say to him, 'Go get 'em, Willie.' Baseball gives every American boy a chance to excel. Not just to be as good as someone else, but to be better. This is the nature of man and the name of the game. I hope that someday Satchel Paige and Josh Gibson will be voted into the Hall of Fame as symbols of the great Negro players who are not here only because they weren't given the chance."

It was a remarkable comment on a day that ostensibly was Williams', and when I read about it I thought back to the day I disliked him for having ignored us Little Leaguers and then beating our Tigers with his less-than-majestic home run. It took somebody as good as Williams to state unequivocally how good Paige and Gibson were, and because of my link to Williams—again possessing some of his greatness, having seen in person how hard he could hit the ball—I decided that I had some inkling of how well the great Paige and the great Gibson must have played baseball.

The same feeling occurred some ten years later when I began researching a novel that was to become *The Bingo Long Traveling All-Stars and Motor Kings*. One of my first personal contacts with the world of Negro baseball in the pre–Jackie Robinson era was James "Cool Papa" Bell, the gazelle of an outfielder who played for the Pittsburgh Crawfords and the Homestead Grays when those teams were the cream of the Negro Leagues. Bell was a man who had been a teammate of Josh and Satchel, a black player who, within the confines of his day, had done it all.

As I pored through Bell's scrapbooks, listening to his commentary rasped with a voice that needed a lemon to keep it strong, the old magic of the man's era came alive. The hours spent with him and his wife, Clarabelle, and more spent with other former stars, were enough, at least in my mind, to rekindle the times: the line drives and the squeeze plays, the three-two pitches, the headfirst slides of black men playing a segregated game. It was enough to create for me a vision of Josh, his grip, the twitching of his biceps, the crack of his bat against a high fastball.

Still, with everything I learned of Josh, everything I felt for him when his former teammates described his stance, his laughter, and his moods, I felt I wanted to know more. "The black Babe Ruth," people called him, to put him in historical perspective. But so many who knew him and saw both him and Ruth called Ruth "the white Josh Gibson." And so much more is known about Ruth, so much more has been written about him, than Gibson.

There is a temptation to say that one is righting a wrong by giving Gibson the time and attention he deserves. But that claim is a bit too grandiose for my blood. No one could ever right the wrong of the major league color ban. Actually, the prohibition against blacks in big-league baseball was but a spot in the massive blot of racial prejudice that has blanketed this country in one form or another since the Emancipation Proclamation. Such a wrong cannot be atoned for, even though present-day progress has righted many racial wrongs. A celebration of the unsung talents of the Negro Leagues—the victims, if you will, of history—brings little comfort to the few Negro League veterans still alive, or the Cool Papa Bells and Josh Gibsons in their graves. It offers a hollow, self-serving sense of assuaged guilt to whites whether or not they participated in the era. A look at the life of Josh Gibson tells us about personality, character, talent: a man's survival and failure in a different age. Only that.

Josh also happened to have lived in a fascinating baseball era, and the remembrance of it serves to bring out the dynamics of those who experienced the times with him, men who also fought the odds. He's been gone fifty years now, his salad days gone sixty, and there simply are few people left who knew what he was like back then. The black experience of a half-century ago invites scrutiny on every level, for not enough of it was chronicled. Even in a sport like baseball, where statistics are kept and memorized with stupefying fastidiousness, records of the Negro Leagues were haphazardly assembled if at all. It has taken modern-day baseball historians exhaustive study of weekly black newspapers and individual scrapbooks to come up with a semblance of an organized record book, and even then much has been lost or simply never recorded. So-called official eyes were never trained on the Negro Leagues, a blindness which did not say that the game or its stars didn't exist, just that they didn't count for very much.

There is an element of romance, of myth, surrounding the home-run hitter, the cleanup man, the big, self-assured superman who comes to the rescue at the late stages, that intoxicates us all. And Josh Gibson, if only in silent black-and-white photographs, brings it alive, a tension that says salvation is at hand. Baseball is one of the few games with that potential for drama, of silent pockets of anticipation before the deliverer saunters up to the plate, waves his club, and rescues everyone from certain destruction.

Josh was almost a superhuman personification of such deliverance, a silent basher who could hit any pitcher, any pitch, at any time, and save the day. He was all of that, and none of it: a human being, an uneducated ball player, a black man, a remarkable specimen of a different era.

He also died just days after his thirty-fifth birthday—not a long life for a man with such talents, but enough of one to inflame the imaginations of many baseball fans and many potential baseball players, black and white. So, in a sense, this look at Gibson is an incomplete picture, simply because it deals primarily with a period of only about twenty years in his life. Those were years in which Josh spent most of his time trying to hit a round ball, trying to perfect the playing of a game. It was a life that left out a chance for much education or culture; his early death came before he had even hit middle age, before he had had time to change with the times or form a perspective of what he had done and who he was.

That perspective had to come from others, mostly those who played with Josh, who traveled with him, ate the same food, fought the same obstacles, had the same skin color. Upon publication of *The Bingo Long Traveling All-Stars and Motor Kings*, many people described the book as "the black *Boys of Summer*," a reference to Roger Kahn's intriguing memoir of the Brooklyn Dodgers. *Bingo Long* really wasn't anything like Kahn's work, but the comparison was flattering. The blacks of Josh Gibson's day were not very much like Kahn's Dodgers other than the fact that they played the same game. The Dodgers were big leaguers. They traveled in trains and ate good food. They got old and had to live with their disillusionment, middle age, and, for some, bad luck.

The blacks of the Negro Leagues seldom could afford the luxury of being disillusioned about anything. They were too busy surviving, trying to play enough games to earn a living wage, wondering what team they would be playing next month, or if that team would even show up to play. Only many years later did the Negro League players look back and wonder what they were thinking about, and how they could have loved the game so much, the same game that pays their grandchildren millions of dollars, yet which some of those same kids consider no fun, the same game that paid them next to nothing at all.

Most of them are gone now. It is left to those of us who caught up with them before they passed away to communicate how spry and alive and vital they were, how they lit up with memories of those bad, good old days, how they replayed doubleheaders in small towns and big cities and hook slid into home plate as if it had all happened the day before yesterday. And the lies—how they guffawed and slapped their thighs at the lies they told. To their dying days, all the veterans of the Negro Leagues were amazed at what they did. They were genuinely likable, gentle, pleasant men. Few had any wealth to speak of, and none had any bloated notion of self-worth. Talking to them was indeed a dialogue with the black boys of summer. I was lucky to have had the privilege.

JOSH GIBSON

1

Up from Buena Vista

Many of them came from the South, the sons of sharecroppers or migrant workers who had been born in the nineteenth century and knew an existence only a barefooted step away from slavery. By 1900, life for Southern blacks had been stripped of the illusions of Reconstruction and had settled into an almost somnolent subservience to the white law of the land. That meant that they got paid for their work, but little else; that life was not slavery, but it was sixty- or seventy-hour weeks of field labor for piddling wages, a reality of day-to-day subsistence which provided little optimism, little hope, and not many good times.

As they had done as slaves, Southern blacks reveled mostly in church, preferring to spend what energy they still had after a week's work in service to the spiritual, the supernatural. If things were hell in the sunshine and dirt of the fields, perhaps they were heaven in the sky, in a life after death that wasn't hot or hard.

Even for the kids there wasn't time for much else, even though at picnics or in the late sun of evening they played baseball. It was a country game which needed only a ball and a bat. Bare hands and bare feet hardened by field work hardly noticed the slap of a ball or the sharp end of a rock in a base path. Most of the games were pickup, friendly, loose affairs with no beginning or end. But occasionally the teams became better organized, the competition keen, and superb athletes—whether they were seven or seventeen—showed their skills. Sometimes the teams became such favorites that women sewed uniforms out of work shirts, and the little boys wore them with style. But it was the South, and few people watched field hands playing baseball in bare feet. Heroics were momentary, heroes celebrated privately within the cheers of the group, a backslap, a hefty slice of cake. There was too much work to be done, too many stomachs to be filled to dally away the time with leisure sports or to unduly celebrate their heroes.

Still, many of those long-legged little boys zealously played the game. In Starkville, Mississippi, in the middle of a dusty field behind shacks, a skinny, bandy-legged kid named James Bell threw blue darters left-handed, once being placed not in the boys' game that he was used to but in the adult contest where thick-handed batters walloped drives into the tall grass and behind the trees. But James Bell, the long-necked thrower with the captivating smile, came into the game, his arm but ten years old, and threw fastballs past the toughest old men around. The ladies chattered and cackled; the little boys closed in and thumped James Bell on the back; the grown men hoisted him on their shoulders and said, "Boy, you're one fine baseball player!"

And James Bell smiled and remembered the moment better than any other and knew in his heart that nothing was more fun and more pleasing and perhaps easier than playing that game. He knew nothing at the time of other little boys with long arms and fearless egos in other Southern fields who were feeling the same magical pride. A boy named Leroy Paige was doing it in Mobile, Alabama; another, named James Crutchfield, though he was tiny and moved like a bug, did it in Ardmore, Missouri. In Buena Vista, Georgia, it was happening to a squat, chunky boy with quick legs and strong wrists, a boy named Joshua Gibson after his grandfather. None of them, not Bell, Paige, Crutchfield, or Gibson, knew of each other, or, for that matter, of much about life beyond those hangdog Southern towns.

They also had no concept of the game of baseball as being

anything other than a game, a breakaway for little boys, a picnic attraction on Sundays. Unlike kids who would play the same game thirty years later in identical sandlots with the same taunts and technique, they did not see baseball as something with a future in it. Southern black kids had no baseball cards with pictures of black baseball professionals. They had few radios and no television sets to show them the game played any other way than as they did it in a dusty field. Only occasionally, in the spring or late fall, a touring team of black professionals chanced through, sometimes stopping and putting on an exhibition, but mostly moving on to bigger things in places like New Orleans, Birmingham, or Atlanta. Places like Starkville or Buena Vista were left with their barren realities and bleak futures, and kids like James Bell and Joshua Gibson saw their feats treasured only in their own memories and exaggerated and passed along by no one.

Mark Gibson was possessed by no visionary impulse when he decided he had to get his family out of Buena Vista, Georgia. Shortly after the turn of the century it became painfully apparent to black leaders and journalists that there was no American Dream to be found for blacks in the South. Some called it unfit for habitation and railed that slavery had been abolished in theory only. Blacks continued to reap few or none of the benefits of industrial growth or economic expansion; they lived in shacks outside of white sections of towns and bore the brunt of an apartheid that knew few variances.

The answer for many was migration to Northern cities, particularly those industrial centers which needed manpower to meet increasing demands for steel, automobiles, and other goods and products that manufacturers were turning out with more and better efficiency. Once they got there, blacks reveled not in their newfound freedom—for racial separation and oppression took other forms—but in the realization of a new future, a new self-dependence fueled by fatter paychecks and more jobs. The call began to go out, usually from black newspapers like the Chicago *Defender,* the New York *Amsterdam News,* the Pittsburgh *Courier,* to blacks who hadn't taken the trek north. By 1915, the migration was in full swing. Railway lines set up direct routes to Chicago, Pittsburgh, Youngstown, Ohio, New York City, Cleveland. And blacks came with everything they owned to take a stab at a new life. In 1917 alone, 65,000 blacks came to Chicago—at the peak hours, 2,000 blacks got off the trains every other day—and prepared to discover for themselves if the Northern dream that their black leaders boasted of really had something to it.

Migrating Southern blacks came not only to cities with more and different jobs, but they came into black communities where they encountered a new vitality. Big-city black publications unceasingly examined the lot of blacks in America. They complained, chided, cajoled, crusaded, and criticized discrimination wherever they found it. The papers were surprisingly vigorous and aggressive, published weekly, and while a handful of copies occasionally trickled down to Southern towns—and were in many places banned from sale or distribution—thousands of copies were sold and read in the big Northern cities every week.

The newspapers' scope was unlimited; their reporting, while often sketchy and inaccurate, was extensive and served to give blacks a sense of unity with their fellows all over the country. The papers popularized causes and grievances, screaming, for example, against lynchings and the conditions in the South which fostered them. Headlines were lurid and damning, and complemented by photos or artists' drawings of ragged blacks swinging from tree limbs. Much of the unceasing reportage of lynchings virtually scooped white newspapers, which, for the most part, ignored the phenomenon. But papers like the *Courier* and the *Defender* kept count, a total which to them was much more grim and shocking than the body count of dead gangsters kept by some white newspapers. Lynchings were abhorred, no matter what form they took. When the state of Alabama began using the electric chair for capital punishment, the Chicago *Defender* featured an editorial cartoon showing a dead black woman in the chair and a smiling, caricatured Alabama official saying, "Since they're making such a fuss about lynchings, I guess I'll do it this way."

The *Defender* once went after an amusement park game it felt was peculiarly degrading to blacks. Called "the African Dodger," the game was popular in traveling carnivals all across the country. It consisted of a black person sitting on a stool, serving as a target for balls thrown at his head. As white patrons lined up, barkers screamed, "Hit the coon and win a cigar!" The *Defender* called the game a disgrace and scolded blacks who hired out for it as being criminal against their race. "We'll go the barker one better," an editorial said in criticism of black "dodgers," and say, "Kill the fool and win a prize!"

Few black people had ever raised such thoughts or voiced them so blatantly to Mark Gibson when he was a sharecropper in Buena Vista. He found life different in Pittsburgh. In 1921, he was but one of a host of Southern blacks who went to that town, then called "the Smoky City," to try to hook on in the steel mills. He was not dreaming, for he shortly found work in the massive Carnegie-Illinois Steel plant. It was a grueling job, but better money than he had ever made in Georgia. Three years later, he sent for his family.

By then there were three children: Josh, born on December 21, 1911; a second son, Jerry, who was born in 1914; and a daughter, Annie, born in 1917. With their mother, Nancy, the former Nancy Woodlock, the kids piled on board a train and were never to see Buena Vista again. It did not bother them, for though Pittsburgh was hardly their idea of a New Land, its Pleasant Valley neighborhood on the city's North Side was an alive, exciting place which offered them more than Buena Vista ever had.

Almost everything in Pittsburgh sloped naturally to the city's center and the three rivers that joined there. It was an awkward, hilly place, inconvenient and difficult to move around in because you had to slavishly follow the rivers until a bridge allowed you to travel laterally from one area to the next. North across the Allegheny from Pittsburgh's downtown was the Pleasant Valley section, with its steep hills and winding streets and houses built right up to the sidewalks. The streets were natural strips for kids, either on foot or on roller skates. Only weeks after the Gibsons got settled on the North Side, Joshua, then twelve and a healthy, strapping boy, got a pair of roller skates and glided up and down the Valley's streets.

He had gone to school in Buena Vista, finished the fifth grade there, but had received only the rudiments of an elementary education. In Pittsburgh he continued in the Allegheny Pre-Vocational School and was guided into electrical studies. But Joshua's life was in the streets and the playgrounds, for, as he got into his teen-age years, his athletic skills developed almost as rapidly as his body. Though stocky and thick-legged, he was a terrifically fast runner and often won track ribbons. He was also a swimmer and established his skills in meets in neighborhood pools. But baseball, the same game he'd played sparingly in Georgia, held a golden appeal for Josh, and in pickup games he grabbed the nearest bat and began swatting pitches with all his might.

Apart from offering a tough, eager Southern boy a chance to play neighborhood sports, Pittsburgh and its North Side transformed Josh in ways he wasn't even aware of. Sports and competition became a prominent thing in his life, an important measure of skill, finesse, competitiveness, and savvy. There was little of that in Georgia, little of the rivalry, the keen edges automatically honed by rubbing against so many others who were also good, or new contests which kept the challenges from fading.

The city also introduced the big time, the professional world of sports that didn't exist in rural Georgia but which was a source of constant, covetous attention for kids in Pittsburgh.

Even if you were black in 1924 in Pittsburgh, Pennsylvania, you could hope to play baseball, a game, as a profession. It was a job that could earn you money and respect and fame among the thousands of kids in Pleasant Valley. There were still no baseball cards or television sets with black stars in them, but there *were* black stars. And boys like Josh widened their horizons as they never had thought possible in Ardmore or Starkville or Buena Vista when they saw their idols in matching uniforms inside spacious parks. It was a very meager slice of the American Dream, but it was a slice. It appeared in the form of a team known as the Homestead Grays.

Located just east of Pittsburgh along the Monongahela River, the small town of Homestead throve and suffered with the awesome steel mills which dominated it. Soot-laden and choked with sulfurous smoke, embroiled intermittently in vicious labor strikes, Homestead in 1911 was also the home of steelworkers who played superb baseball. The best of them played for the Murdock Grays, an integrated team—though mostly black—which competed against and usually beat most other teams in Pittsburgh's steel-producing valleys.

The Grays were transformed in 1911, however, when they were joined by a light-skinned, thin-faced boy just back from college at Penn State. His name was Cumberland Willis Posey, "Cum" to his teammates, and in a matter of two years he became captain of the Grays, then known as the Homestead Grays, and worked at organizing them into a semiprofessional team.

Posey was a cunning player, and a literate if dictatorial manager. He pushed the team into playing more and better baseball, fought against a crusty Pennsylvania ban against Sunday games—one which he finally saw reversed, in time to give a financial boost to the team—and by 1922 had finally put players on salary. The first Gray to get paid was Charles "Lefty" Williams, a pitcher. But another pitcher named Wil-

liams—"Smokey Joe" Williams, who had established a brilliant
reputation with black teams in New York and Chicago, was
added to the payroll in 1925. It was Smokey Joe Williams's
signing that started Cum Posey's Grays toward the big time, and
even though they did not belong to an established Negro league,
they soon were the most prominent black team in Pennsylvania.

Under Posey's cool, disciplined business hand, the Grays
began making money in the late 1920s. Posey possessed one of
the best baseball minds in the country and knew talent as well as
any man. His teams were filled with top players, and the fans
around Pittsburgh—black and white alike—knew it. They
turned out by the thousands at Forbes Field, the home of the
major-league Pittsburgh Pirates, which Posey rented when the
Pirates were out of town. When they weren't at home, the Grays
traveled to neighboring mining and steel towns and played the
tough, well-stocked local teams.

The Posey brand of baseball was a methodical, no-nonsense
game which approached major-league caliber. The Grays were
an efficient, almost colorless team, dressed in their plain white
uniforms with the large-lettered "GRAYS" or just a single "G"
across the front, which played the game well, usually won, and
made money. By doing it, they became heroes to the fans and the
kids of Homestead and Pittsburgh, kids like Josh Gibson, and
became known as the Yankees of Pittsburgh black baseball.
They were strong every year, uncompromising, cool, and very,
very good. Cum Posey made it clear that he wouldn't tolerate it
any other way.

Throughout most of the 1920s, Posey had little to do with
organized black baseball. That was largely the creation of the
notorious Rube Foster of Chicago, a former standout pitcher
who had turned to organizing and owning teams in Chicago just
after the turn of the century. At that time, baseball, both black
and white versions, was played by hundreds of teams in sandlot
leagues, industrial leagues, neighborhood and community
leagues. (It was not uncommon for major-league players to

moonlight on these teams, even during the regular season, in order to pick up a few extra dollars.) In 1911, Foster, after a career mainly with the Chicago Union Giants and Chicago's Leland Giants, formed the Chicago American Giants, a black team, which, under his direction, became a powerhouse.

But Foster's ambition was to organize a Negro league on the scale of a major-league enterprise, made up of established black teams from the big Northern cities. In 1920 he proposed a league with Eastern and Midwestern divisions, each with at least eight clubs. Only one division got off the ground. Officially known as the Negro National League, it consisted of Foster's American Giants, the Cuban Stars, Dayton Marcos, Chicago Giants, Detroit Stars, Indianapolis ABCs, Kansas City Monarchs, and St. Louis Giants.

Though plagued by a stumbling start, shaky franchises, and an uncertain schedule, Foster's NNL managed to survive. With Rube running it almost single-handedly, the league maintained itself as none before it ever had.

In 1923, a group of owners formed the Eastern Colored League. With teams from Brooklyn, New York, Baltimore, and Philadelphia, the Eastern League had no desire to combine with Foster's NNL. Instead, it openly competed with it, fighting for players and franchises. As a result, both leagues teetered perilously close to collapse throughout most of the decade.

Well aware of the leagues' fiscal shortcomings and general instability, Cum Posey kept his Homestead Grays out of both circuits. Not only did he disapprove of the way the leagues were run, but Posey also felt his own control of the Grays would be undercut by the demands of the parent organizations. He had a good thing going with the Grays as independents, and as much as either league would have welcomed a franchise as established as Homestead, Posey saw no reason to jeopardize his success in order to aid other, less efficient managements. He also had an ego the size of Rube Foster's, and that of Nat Strong, the power of the Eastern League, and did not wish to take on either man.

Foster faded, however, while only in his forties, not from business setbacks but from mental illness. By 1926, after having guided the American Giants so forcefully and given the needed organizational push to the Negro leagues, Rube was unable to function from day to day. In September of that year, the Chicago *Tribune* carried a report of Foster's arrest for attacking a friend and attempting to stab him with an ice pick. He was jailed and appeared in front of Judge Irving L. Weaver in what was then known in Chicago as Psychopathic Court. Weaver judged him insane and committed him to the Kankakee Asylum in that south Chicago suburb.

Despite the reported attack, Foster's relatives insisted he was harmless, though no longer acting or thinking sanely. His wife told police that Rube suffered severe delusions, especially one in which "a World Series was in progress and he was needed to pitch." He remained hospitalized for four years until, at the age of fifty-one, on December 9, 1930, he died.

Without Foster, the Negro National League fell apart, finally folding in 1932. The F. .tern League had collapsed earlier, failing to complete the 1928 season. In its place, a league known as the American Negro League was organized. It was with this league that Posey finally decided to bring his Grays into organized baseball, and their presence in the league was the beginning of Posey's impressive political influence on all of Negro baseball.

Posey had his problems, not the least of which was his attempt to inject stability into league franchises battered by the new hard times of the Depression. The American Negro League soon folded, its clubs drifting to other leagues or forming new ones in a confusing jumble, and a new Negro National League emerged. In it were teams from the East and Midwest, including the Grays, clubs strong enough for the most part to keep the new league in business.

On the baseball side of the Grays, Posey continued to sign top-caliber players to complement Smokey Joe Williams, Vic

Harris, and Martin Dihigo, a Cuban considered one of the best Negro league players in the country. The Grays were undisputed masters of Pennsylvania baseball, and their many games in Forbes Field were exciting attractions in Pittsburgh, events witnessed by thousands and which never failed to light up the skies in the minds of the little black boys who watched.

Josh stayed in Allegheny Pre-Vocational until he was sixteen and had finished ninth grade. He began to work in an air-brakes manufacturing plant as an apprentice, a job that gave way to one in the steel mills, and another in a downtown department store. Besides being physically powerful, Josh was a good worker, an even-tempered, likable teen-ager who never created problems. He wasn't precocious or intellectual, nor was he raised in a household that stressed learning. A family fresh from the South as the Gibsons was more interested in getting by, and Josh, like most boys his age, was expected to hold his own.

As early as 1927 he had begun to make his name as a sandlot ballplayer. He played first for a North Side team called the Pleasant Valley Red Sox, then for the Gimbels A.C., an all-black recreation team. He was a catcher even then, a position that seemed natural for him because of his size and his strength, and also because of his quickness. He played the next year for the Crawford Colored Giants, a team he helped organize, along with Harry Beale, a well-known North Side player and manager.

The Crawfords were a cut above most sandlot teams. The best young ballplayers in Pittsburgh played for it, including Josh and a light-skinned pitcher named Harry Kincannon. Though they couldn't compete with the likes of the Homestead Grays, the Craws were big favorites and drew nice crowds. Considered a semipro team, they played most of their games at Ammon Field on the North Side. A hat was usually passed, and out of the meager donations came expenses and a few bucks a day for the players. It wasn't a flourishing operation, but the team got around and made a name against the best of the semipro teams around the Pittsburgh area. They rated a mention now and again in the Pittsburgh *Courier*, usually on sports pages dominated by headlines made by the Grays.

Times were still booming in the American economy, and they spilled over to the black communities. A kid as good as Josh could look to baseball for his livelihood, for the teams were plentiful, games more so—the Crawford Giants played as many as a hundred games in a summer season—and fans were flushed with enough change to make it worthwhile. Still, there was no letup on the part of black leaders who believed things could be a lot better. The *Courier* in Pittsburgh lashed out at businesses which had brisk black patronage but no black employees. "They take our dollars with smiling faces/But hire no Negroes in their places," read one editorial cartoon. With its slogan, "Covering the Country Like a Tent," the *Courier* aimed not to relax until things improved.

Sports pages remained a prime ingredient of black newspapers, with entertainment sections close competitors. Black stars, while making their names all over the country, were doted on when they showed up in town. A comer in 1930 was Louis Armstrong, but even his rise was not without an occasional setback. That year a *Courier* headline blared, LOUIS ARMSTRONG ARRESTED IN DOPE SCANDAL, and went on to report that Louis had been charged in Culver City, California, with "possession of dope, the kind used in cigarets." Armstrong was booked and released on bail, and ultimately avoided prosecution, but the *Courier* in its wry style of communicating the obvious to its readers, took the occasion to comment, "Armstrong is known all over the country for his 'high' notes on the cornet."

Courier readers, *Defender* readers, and others in black communities all over the country hardly had to be instructed on the trends of the times and the way black people adapted to them. There was enough money around in the 1920s for many blacks to stay in style, to live a little, especially when a suit cost only

$22.50, haircuts a dime. The rakes among the men worked at keeping their hair straight, some relying on "Mme. C. J. Walker's Nifty Fit Cap," which could be worn day or night and came with or without a detachable sun shade. "Throw away the old unsightly stocking cap," Mme. Walker advertised. "Avoid embarrassment of asking sister, mother, wife, or aunt for a discarded hose. Goodness gracious man, your hair will be sleek, straight, and silky." It came in orange with a black circular stripe. Only fifty cents.

The ball game was as good a place as any to strut one's stuff and show off a wardrobe. In Yankee Stadium on the Fourth of July weekend in 1930, ladies in summer dresses and men in various-colored berets came for the holiday sounds of the 369th Regiment Army band and to watch entertainer Bill "Bojangles" Robinson (who was later to own a part of a New York Negro team) race a group of kids in the hundred-yard dash. Bojangles, however, ran it backward. It was good enough summer entertainment to attract 20,000 people, one of whom came in a tuxedo coat, an aviation collar and batwing tie, carrying a cane, and wearing sport shoes and white flannel trousers.

When the stock market crashed and hard times followed, black communities and their baseball were hit even harder than their white counterparts. Teams like the Crawford Giants suffered, especially since their revenues came mostly from donations. In 1930, fans were supposed to pay a nickel a head to watch the games at Ammon Field, but most dropped in pennies or nothing at all. Such cheapness was a scandal, sportswriters claimed. It was really nothing of the sort, nor was it necessarily a comment on the brand of baseball being played. North Side Pittsburgh blacks were simply growing hard-pressed for cash. They hadn't lost their appreciation of the game, and they hadn't stopped showing up, but they simply couldn't afford to spare a dime.

By the summer of 1930, Josh was hitting baseballs out of parks all over Pittsburgh as the Colored Giants' regular catcher.

His exploits occasionally appeared in the *Courier* much to the delight of his father, and particularly his mother, Nancy, who had come to love baseball and her son's ability to play it. They didn't mind that his name was sometimes spelled "Gipson" in the *Courier*, for it was a mistake not often to be repeated. With each game he played, fewer and fewer people who knew baseball in Pennsylvania remained unaware of who Josh Gibson was or what he could do. That included the management of the Grays over in Homestead.

In 1930, Cum Posey, with the financial support of co-owner Charlie Walker, put together the best Homestead Gray team ever. Coming out of a long, grimy winter, in a place where the snow stayed white only hours before the smokestacks turned it grainy and gray, ball fans looked forward to sitting in the cheap seats, kicking out their legs, and watching lazy fly balls and screaming liners. The Grays first headed South, to Hot Springs, Arkansas, then over to Louisiana for spring training. It would be a few weeks before they worked their way back to Pittsburgh to do their stuff.

They took off in two cars, two new Buicks, bought with money made by Posey and Charlie Walker in past seasons. The autos well suited a team with the likes of Oscar Charleston, a first baseman fast becoming the most effective ballplayer in Negro baseball; Vic Harris, a tough outfielder-catcher; Smokey Joe Williams; catcher Buck Ewing; and third baseman Judy Johnson. It was mid-March, and the hot waters and warm breezes of Arkansas were a welcome change from western Pennsylvania. The players were loose and they enjoyed the small towns and pressure-free baseball. The only concern in these months was that they were in the South, and they well knew it every minute of the day.

In only a few Southern towns did teams like the Grays relax. One was Monroe, Louisiana, a village that loved its baseball and treated visiting Northern teams like royalty. The owner of the

Monroe Monarchs was J. C. Stovall, a white businessman who believed Monroe's black people were as important as its whites. He not only built a fine ball park but added a swimming pool and dance area, and three-room bungalows for his players and their families. Stovall even went so far one year as to work out a situation in which a ballplayer who was in jail for murder was released on weekends to pitch for the team. Black ballplayers said it and said it often: if they had to choose to live in any place in the South, it would be in J. C. Stovall's Monroe.

Once out of Monroe, however, black teams hit places like Jackson, Mississippi, where they knew they wouldn't be able to buy gas, or use the washrooms, or eat a meal. Jackson was a place to be entered at night and left that same night, for there was no sense in fighting the name calling, the epithets about being "Northern niggers." The fact that they might be the powerful Grays meant nothing in Jackson in 1930, as it didn't in many other towns. In Lumberton and Laurel, Mississippi, the merchants wouldn't sell them white milk or ice cream. In Cleveland, Mississippi, the team was once in town when a group of men grabbed a small black boy trying to get air for his bicycle tire, put the hose into his rectum, and blew him to pieces. In such places there was no sense in sticking around, in pushing things.

There wasn't time to make trouble, anyway, for spring training also meant playing two and three games a day from Hot Springs, Arkansas, to New Orleans, then back north through Kentucky, over to St. Louis, then back to Pittsburgh.

The miles were long and tough, even in the Grays' two new Buicks. Judy Johnson still laughs about the day the two cars turned over within ten miles of each other. On the way to Shreveport, Louisiana, the cars, each with nine men inside, racks on the sides to hold clothes, and a box on the back with equipment, raced each other to get to town first in order to get the best hotel rooms. Oscar Charleston was driving the lead car and he was turning up so much dust that Charlie Walker in the second car couldn't see a thing. The roads were built with deep ditches on each side and were graded periodically so that a knoll of dirt was left in the middle. Walker hit the knoll, lost control of the car, and struggled wildly while the Buick bounced from side to side, went into the ditch, and turned over. Despite the crowd and the load, nobody was hurt. The car never stopped running, and with a slightly twisted fender, it was pushed upright and carried the team on down the road.

About ten minutes later, it came upon another car, also in the ditch.

"Look at that poor bastard," Charlie Walker said. "Did the same thing we did."

Then they realized it was Charleston and the rest of the Grays. They had blown a tire, hit the knoll-and-ditch combination, and turned over three times. Most of the passengers were thrown out through the canvas top of the Buick and landed unhurt in the grass. Charleston came up with the steering wheel in pieces in his hands, for the wooden wheel had shattered as he fought to hold onto it. Splinters from the wheel were lodged in his scalp so deeply that they stayed there for days until he could get to a town with a doctor good enough to get them out.

The team made it to Shreveport, as they made it to all of their stops that spring despite the bad food and the long miles that made their ankles swell, and lodgings that were sometimes so bug-ridden that players preferred to sleep sitting in chairs.

By April they were back in Pittsburgh: the formidable Homestead Grays. The summer game once again returned. Sportswriters described the event as grandly as they could. "King baseball," one wrote, "the crown head of all that is sportive, will return to the North Side this Saturday afternoon."

To fans, the Grays were cast as more than mere ballplayers, overgrown boys playing a stick-and-ball sport; they were *personalities* who plied trades and developed skills equal to those of prizefighters or biblical heroes or soldiers in battle. Catchers were called "mask artists"; a fearsome pitcher was labeled a "stormy petrel." An April exhibition game against an All-Star team earned this buildup: "The starting lineup of the All-Stars will begin with a host of players well-known to the fans. Sweatt is to play center field. Bray will catch. Hines will take care of second base. 'Jew Baby' Bennett will look pleasant in left field. Torrienti of the Gilkersons will mind the initial sack. Hayes will prance on third base. Boisy Marshall, who last year played a couple of games with the Giants, will smile on shortstop."

Yet, as creatively as the sportswriters stocked their prose, and as fondly as fans looked upon baseball in 1930, the game that spring was hard-pressed to remain in business. League teams were impoverished, schedules light and uncertain. Players were criticized for being pampered and unprofessional, out of condition and unmotivated.

"Candy Jim" Taylor, the outspoken manager of the Memphis Red Sox who had spent most of his life around Negro baseball, complained at the start of the 1930 season that most players didn't care enough to stay in shape. "The most they care for is the 1st and the 15th of the month when payday rolls around," Taylor wrote. He went on to suggest that Negro baseball as started by Rube Foster ten years before was on its last legs, not only because of weak owners but also because of bad umpires or umpires paid by the team instead of the league, lack of publicity, dirty ball parks, and unclean uniforms.

"The 1929 season was the poorest from standpoints of both playing and attendance since the beginning of the Negro National League in 1920," Taylor concluded.

Another writer said that Negro baseball was in need of a housecleaning. "I have seen players walk off the playing field to take a drink of bootleg whiskey from the bottle of some rowdy fan, and they use profane language in front of the stands where the fans may hear it."

Yet nobody suggested the games shouldn't go on, or that they would not. From city to city, teams and franchises varied enormously in fiscal and physical prowess. Few owners kidded themselves about the new hard times of 1930, but they differed in their attitudes on what to do about them. Some would fold before putting up much of a fight. Others would sign new ballplayers, book more games, sink money into new ball parks, even invest in portable lighting systems which, for the first time ever, would bring about nighttime baseball.

There were few things in the game, however, which brought people into the ball parks in 1930 as well as a genuine star. In the spring of that year, a kid who would become one of the game's biggest was awaiting his chance. King baseball had returned to the Smoky City. It wouldn't be long now.

2

A Homestead Gray

The game is so complex because it rewards so early. Baseball is one of the few games which are not dominated by physical strength or size, but by dexterity. It involves a quickness, particularly of the hands, in reflex coordination with the eyes. That is why it is not uncommon to see a very young boy master many of the techniques of the game, much of its execution, with a fluidity and grace that result when the body is perfectly in tune with its reflexes. I have watched ten-year-old catchers perform all of the moves of that position and do so effortlessly, even though it is a position which makes endless physical and mental demands. At few times in its development is the human body as dexterous as when it is ten years old, before it begins the often awkward teen-age growth. Add to this a kid's relentless devotion to learning baseball, and the result is a physical package perfectly suited to the game. The same cannot be said for a lot of other sports—not football with its accent on strength and a ball which few subteen-agers can even throw; not basketball with its difficult moves, its emphasis on height, and its even bigger ball; not golf; not tennis; nor any other sport which requires some mastery of an unwieldy piece of equipment.

I know that partly because I was a truly gifted ten-year-old ballplayer. There is no doubt in my mind that I was better at the game then, a more fearless, more aggressive, faster player than I was after that, even though I was awarded most-valuable-player trophies in high school and college. I don't think I ever again hit the ball so proportionately hard or far or handled a glove so well as I did as a Little Leaguer, and I was haunted always by the possibility that I had peaked too soon. I was told by a casual acquaintance after my eleven-year-old season that such things happened, that some players were better in Little League than ever again in their lives, and they realized it only years later.

A lot of shadows come into the picture once a kid grows out of his adolescent baseball spikes. The world becomes bigger, the game much smaller, so much so that by high school a tough Little Leaguer seldom has much zeal for the game left in him. And it is at that time, when a ballplayer goes from age thirteen to age seventeen, that his career as a player is pretty much decided. If he loses the coordination, the speed, the agility that he had as a kid, he is through. If he keeps it all, but doesn't grow physically strong, he is just as through. And it all comes to bear in a short time. When a kid is sixteen he should be able to play with men; by the time he is nineteen he will be as physically developed and as able to play the game as at any other time in his life. It is then that the pros decide on his fate and persuade themselves that a kid can take on the polish which will make him able to compete with the best.

Josh would go anywhere to find a ball game, to hang on the screen behind the plate and watch the angles, study the moves. He was only a kid, but long past the stage in which a home run or a classy double play impressed him. He wasn't looking for such things. He watched players when they didn't have the ball, when it wasn't anywhere near them, and he would watch how they concentrated, how they broke, how they reacted to tiny movements from others. Mostly he was interested in execution, the countless movements which made up the play.

He watched catchers: how they squatted, how they threw, how they called pitches, talked to the infield, chattered with batters, argued with umpires, received pitches, chased foul flies, blocked low pitches. He was fascinated and made mental pictures, took endless mental notes. It was, after pitching, the single most difficult position to master on the baseball field, and there was never any doubt in his mind that he was a catcher and would be one for a long time to come.

Hitting was another thing, and he studied hitters almost as much as catchers. But hitting didn't concern or trouble him. He felt better with a bat in his hand than with anything else, that supreme feeling of waiting to hit, then walking into the box, the eyes, the focus of everyone in the ball park and everyone in the field on him. It was a power he relished, a skill he possessed naturally. Hitting was a matter of putting wood against the ball, and no matter how you did it, whether or not you stepped away or into the ball, fell back or lunged, swung hard or poked, the final result was all that mattered. There was no reward in a perfect swing or perfect batting form if the ball didn't shoot past the infielders. If it did, nobody cared what you looked like doing it.

So as soon as the weather broke and the teams banded, he played often and looked for other games to watch. He was big and strong, now 190 pounds of muscle spread on a six-foot, two-inch frame, with solid, muscular legs as fast as a sprinter's. As hard as he studied others and tried to pick up tips, it mattered only marginally, for every bone in his body was made for the game. Even though Josh was only eighteen, few persons alive were so naturally superb at it as he was.

The story of how he joined the Homestead Grays has had many versions through the years, most of them embellished to befit the career that followed. The tale most commonly told—and, unfortunately, the one farthest from the truth—puts Josh in the stands during a game between the Grays and one of the premier Negro teams, the Kansas City Monarchs. It was not a commonplace mid-July game at Forbes Field, but rather a sensational new phenomenon, for the Monarchs came into town with their own portable lighting system. Besides their bus, they traveled with twelve trucks carrying a 250-horsepower engine for a generator and towers with clusters of lights that were placed on the perimeter of the playing field. It was by no means a piece of lighting perfection, for the poles were not very tall and the lights capable only of putting out illumination which in the minds of the players was just better than candles. Added to that was a generator that coughed and sputtered, causing the lights to dim annoyingly. It also was easy to hit a ball above the lights into the pitch blackness of the night sky, and when this happened, the fielders wandered around like bugs trying to figure out when and where the ball would come back into sight.

But the drawbacks of the lighting system were minimal compared to the fact that so many more people were able to attend weeknight games, and they could do so in the cooler air of evening. A Grays-Monarch series would have brought out the fans, anyway, but playing it under the lights was a sure draw.

The story holds that Josh was sitting in a seat near the Grays' dugout eating hot dogs and enjoying the pitching performance of Smokey Joe Williams, who at fifty-four was still one of the Grays' great attractions. The lean, angular Texan with the thin cheekbones was capable of throwing a mean fastball, a holdover from his days at the turn of the century when ballplayers black and white said nobody could throw the thing any faster.

When the game got under way, it was decided by Grays catcher Buck Ewing and Williams that because of the lights only two pitches would be thrown—the fastball and the curve—and that the signals between them would consist only of Ewing's glove held up or held down. It took only a few innings before the two of them became crossed up, and Ewing caught a pitch on his bare hand, splitting a finger. He was unable to go on, and Cum Posey looked to Vic Harris, a versatile outfielder, to take over. Harris refused, however, saying that he couldn't see well enough in the artificial light to catch Williams.

That left Posey with no alternative. When he spotted Josh sitting in the back of the dugout, he decided that the young boy's wide, massive face and strong shoulders were the picture of willingness. The request was made, and even though Josh was supposedly dressed in the work clothes he wore to his job at the Edgar Thomson steel mills, he jumped at the offer. "Oh, yeah!" he is said to have hollered when Posey asked him if he'd catch the rest of the game.

What followed was the stuff of legend, for the tale has Josh catching most of what Smokey Joe Williams threw, and if he didn't, he positioned himself squarely behind the pitches so that they bounced off his chest. It looked at times as though Williams were throwing against a wall, for what Josh didn't see, he felt. The game went on, the Grays and Williams beat the Monarchs, 6-5, on Vic Harris's home run, and Josh had made an incredible entry into the big time.

Like so many baseball tales, the story is only partially true. It was not like Cum Posey to go into important games unprepared or thin at any position. At that time in the season, he had Ewing as his first-line catcher, and pitcher George Britt and outfielder Vic Harris as backups. Yet Posey was looking for a solid substitute catcher, and Josh's reputation was no secret to him. As he wrote a few years later, Posey contacted Josh and told him to be ready to play for the Grays at any time.

The situation arose not in the midst of a crucial night game before thousands of fans, as the popular story holds, but in a twilight doubleheader against Dormont, a white semipro team. Buck Ewing did split a finger, and Posey put Vic Harris in to catch until Josh could be brought over. Posey then sent Vic's brother by taxi over to Ammon Center, where Josh was playing with the Crawford Giants. The two returned a few innings later, and Josh was unceremoniously put into the Grays' lineup.

The game most often cited as Josh's first with the Grays, the July 25 night contest with the Monarchs, was actually pitched not by Smokey Joe Williams but by Charles "Lefty" Williams, another fine Gray thrower. In that game Josh shared catching duties with Buck Ewing, and each man batted twice.

Josh stayed with the team and spelled Ewing from time to time until he could completely take the job from the veteran receiver. In those first few games with the Grays, including the night games against the Monarchs, Josh was indeed hard-pressed to catch the firing of a variety of Gray pitchers, including Smokey Joe Williams. On more than a few occasions, fastballs bounced off his chest, and curves rattled against his shin guards.

Regardless of how momentous Josh's introduction into big-time Negro baseball actually was—and in years following, Josh would laugh about the story which had him dropping his hot dogs for a catcher's mitt—he was on the Grays to stay. Though his defensive game left room for much improvement, he was most definitely a natural, robust, inflamed young ballplayer who could do nothing but get better, incredibly better.

His rise brought a new world with it, and it took him away from the old. From then on Josh was a professional baseball player. He began a life divorced from his family and hometown friends, for even though the Grays did not travel as extensively during the season as other Negro league teams, Josh and his teammates spent almost every day of the year looking for a game, be it on the West Coast in the fall, Central and South America in the winter, or South in the spring. He came to know his teammates better than his parents, his sister and brother, and he drifted apart from the friends he grew up with on the North Side of Pittsburgh.

He also limited himself to nothing but baseball; if he was not playing the game, he was thinking about it, practicing it, traveling for it. The game gave him a rare chance to see most of the United States and a number of foreign countries. He matured very quickly as far as his ability to get around in new surroundings was concerned, yet he was to be totally sheltered by the game he played and the organization he played for. For the most part, his fellow ballplayers were like him: able to read and write but seldom doing it enough to even send letters home. Rarely did he read a book, study something, or develop new interests. He only occasionally challenged a teammate about social issues or talked about ideas outside of the pale of the game. And even though he had to cope with a fickle social and racial climate in this country, he did not spend much time thinking about it or devising ways to change it. If anything got in the way of playing baseball, he avoided it, for his was a single-minded, stifled life, and he wasn't interested in much more.

Still, for a country kid from southern Georgia, the opportunity Joshua Gibson found as a Homestead Gray outstripped anything he would have dreamed possible as a kid, or that his father while a sharecropper would have imagined for him. Josh was earning his living, and would do it nicely at times, by swinging a bat, something he loved doing. And if a man could earn his bread by doing something he didn't consider work, well, that was a dream. That it took him away from his family or inhibited his ability to expand his learning or develop other skills was a secondary drawback, hardly worth mentioning when compared to the opportunity that had come his way.

The Grays not only kept Josh after that night, they played him as often as possible. Ewing's finger healed soon after, and he resumed most of the catching. Josh came into games in later innings or caught the tail end of doubleheaders. Occasionally he played the outfield, batted sixth or seventh in the strong Gray lineup, and tried to pick up as much as he could as fast as he could. He was overwhelmingly enthusiastic and absorbed with baseball every minute of the day.

He looked to Judy Johnson, even though Judy was close to his own age, as a mentor, and after games at home and on the road, sometimes when Judy was exhausted and barely awake in his hotel room or in the cars, Josh would approach him and say, "Jing?"—for he called Judy that—"what did I do wrong today?" The question came every day, after every game, and Judy, seeing the flat-faced innocence and the raw skill of the teen-ager, couldn't resist spending the time to talk ball, the angles, the strategies, the small moves that Josh still wanted to review, even though he had by then already mastered them.

In no time the black sports press had adopted Josh and started throwing superlatives at him. "Samson Gibson is green but a terrific threat when crouching over the plate with a bat," wrote W. Rollo Wilson of the Philadelphia *Independent*.

It was but the beginning. By September 1930, Wilson was employing prose reminiscent of *Beowulf* and Shakespeare to talk about Gibson.

> . . . well, the kid could catch and did catch and is still catching. He's green yet but the ripening process is moving apace. He has not mastered the technique in throwing to second base but he kills off all the fast boys who try to steal. His stance at the plate is worse than Pimp Young's [another Gray catcher] but he gets his basehits. His motto is—"a homer a day will boost my pay."

Such prose was to mythologize Gibson for the rest of his career. And it was all done in print, filled by the imagination of the sportswriter who could spot a hero when he saw one.

> And strong! Ask any ball player about what a rough playmate Oscar Charleston is. Then ask any Gray athlete how this gawky kid mishandled the Hoosier Hustler on Forbes Field a pair of fortnights back. Cum's young partner, Charlie Walker, calls him Samson.
>
> And eat! That boy has a keener zest for food than does your fat correspondent. He spends more money for "snacks" than any of the other players lavish on three meals. It takes a tremendous amount of fodder to satisfy his growing body and nourish his 194 pounds of bones and muscle.

Wilson didn't have to dig for his descriptions of Josh's physical characteristics, for they were plain to any Gray fan who watched Josh lumber around Forbes Field in his baggy-trousered uniform. Off the field Josh did eat everything in sight, especially quarts of vanilla ice cream whenever he could get his hands on it. He was an important addition to the club not only because he was so good but because his almost childlike enthusiasm infected the other Grays. He was a joy to be around, a terror on the field who looked upon himself, in that first summer of his pro career, as a kid wonderfully placed among his idols.

Sportswriters such as Rollo Wilson also attempted to create a personality for Josh, and at this time in his life, they were flirting with fiction.

They should have named him Josher instead of Joshua, for he sure can kid with the kidders. For confirmation of this you may communicate with the renowned Raleigh Mackey, now laboring for the Baltimore Black Sox. On a recent Sunday in the Monumental City the kid so worked on the perspiring Biz each time he came to bag that he was fit to be tied, as the expression goes.

"Aha!" sneered Gibson, when Mackey clumped out to the plate. "So this is Mr. Mackey, the famous catcher and batter. I've been readin' a lot about you in the papers. I believe you were in the games in Pittsburgh Friday and yesterday. You didn't do so well, did you? Well, you're gonna do worse today.

"Oh, you missed that one! Too bad. Now, sir, here is one right down the alley. What? Only a foul? My fault, sire, I forgot that I had called for one on the inside. Don't hit at this one, it's an off ball. So sorry! The darn fool pitcher crossed you up. His control was bad and he cut the corner. Yes, Mr. Mackey, that was three strikes. You are excused for the time being. Perhaps you will do better the next time; you may hit it to the infield."

As chatty and excited as Josh was behind the plate, such razzing was totally uncharacteristic, especially when he was young. He was too intent on performing the mechanics of the game to outtalk the hitters. He was also greatly intimidated by the veteran catchers such as Mackey, and seldom taunted them as they batted. Instead, he hollered and thumped his glove and rooted the pitcher's deliveries home. He made noise and kept his head in the game. He was too unsure of himself in the summer of 1930 to banter with the veterans. That, too, would come later, when he was much more confident of himself as a catcher and as a star. Yet his badinage would never develop to the point where Josh became known for his quick wit, or his slicing remarks behind the plate. Sportswriters, fans, even owners wished it from him over the years, but it never flowed in any great amount.

Off the field, he continued to haunt Judy Johnson ("Jing? How'd I do today? What'd I do wrong?") with the same relentless devotion to bettering himself. and Johnson, Charleston, Buck Ewing, most of the Gray veterans, talked baseball with him and reviewed games and plays, but knew damn well that they weren't teaching Gibson much he didn't already know or wasn't picking up and adapting to his style with each passing game.

As the season went on, the Grays continued to play impressive baseball and convince most observers that the 1930 team was one of the best ever. On August 9, in a repeat series under the lights with the Monarchs at their own Muehlenbach Field, Smokey Joe Williams beat them 1-0 in twelve innings. He pitched against Chet Brewer, who was also to become one of the finest pitchers in the Negro leagues, and the two of them were untouchable most of the night. Brewer gave up four hits and a run; Williams allowed only one hit and shut out the Monarchs.

A fascinating footnote to that game concerns the colorful and controversial practice of the Negro-league pitchers of doctoring the baseball. For years pitchers acquired extra English in the form of Vaseline, hair tonic, or saliva, or they cut the ball with a fingernail, razor, or bottle cap in a back pocket or under the visor of their caps. More common was the use of an emery cloth, an abrasive cloth used in polishing, which pitchers used to scuff the ball. The "emery ball," a jumping, dipping, unpredictable pitch, became a well-known pitch with many throwers, and though it wasn't declared illegal, arguments over its use frequently came up. Prior to the Gray-Monarch game that night, Cum Posey and Monarch owner J. L. Wilkinson had agreed that neither pitcher would use the emery ball. But when Brewer got into trouble with two men on, he went to his emery cloth (called his "work" by teammates) and pitched out of the jam. Smokey Joe Williams retaliated by taking a sheet of sandpaper to the mound with him, and the battle was on. In the dim, flickering lights, the batters were the predictable victims, and an incredible forty-six of them struck out. Brewer got nineteen with his emery ball; Smokey Joe fanned twenty-seven with his sandpaper.

By the end of the 1930 season, the Grays were attempting to establish their dominance over Negro baseball in the Eastern part of the country. To do it, they took on New York's Lincoln Giants in a ten-game series beginning in late September.

Both teams were strong and solidly coached, and with overwhelming publicity from black papers in both cities, the series attracted a lot of attention. Part of that was due to a remarkable coincidence. Four of the five greatest players in the history of Negro baseball were playing in the series. Josh was finishing out his first summer. Oscar Charleston, the dour first baseman who was generally acknowledged to be the most versatile ballplayer in the game, was in his prime in the middle of the Grays' lineup. Smokey Joe Williams at fifty-four, was still making headlines and establishing his mastery over those who hadn't been around long enough to know that there were few pitchers better than he. And for the Lincoln Giants, a tall, smiling forty-six-year-old shortstop was finishing out his career. He was John Henry Lloyd, a left-handed hitter who for twenty-five years had done it all in organized Negro baseball and become a legend to its fans. By that summer he was called "Pop" Lloyd, and there were few people who took him for granted or let down against him for a minute.

The Grays beat the Giants six out of ten before crowds that ranged from 8,000 to 20,000 in Pittsburgh's Forbes Field and Yankee Stadium in New York. It was in a Yankee Stadium game that Josh crashed a home run to the bullpen in left field— more than 500 feet away—that fans for years after would claim as one of the longest drives ever hit there. Josh was described as a "sensation," in every sense of the word, and every time he connected, sportswriters hunted for new adjectives. And he had yet to turn nineteen.

The year of his brilliant professional debut was also one of personal tragedy. A couple of years before, Josh had met Helen Mason, an attractive, friendly girl from the Hill District. She was only a few months younger than Josh, and as teen-agers the two of them got along well and saw each other regularly. Helen's parents, James and Margaret, had come up to Pittsburgh from the South, as had Josh's mother and father, and they liked the friendly, exuberant, brawny boy their daughter had eyes for.

Helen became pregnant just after her seventeenth birthday, and she and Josh were married. The two of them lived with the Masons on Bedford Avenue in the Hill District. Josh worked at a variety of jobs, but by then baseball was fast becoming his real vocation. As Helen approached her expected delivery date, Josh premiered with the Grays, and it seemed for the beaming boy from Buena Vista that life held nothing but promise.

In August, Helen went into a complicated labor. At Pittsburgh's Magee Hospital, she delivered twin babies, a boy and a girl, but the births brought on convulsions, she lapsed into a coma, and a few hours later her heart gave out and she was dead.

Only the birth of the twins, named Helen and Josh, Jr., lessened the tragedy of Helen's death. Yet Josh, as a fledgling Homestead Gray, was unable to care for his children. They were raised by the Masons, primarily Helen's sisters and her mother, and saw their father only when he came back to town.

The arrangement was to become a source of hard feelings, for Josh, with his success as a pro, was hard-pressed to be a ballplayer and a father. He was seldom home, and when winter came he headed south for valuable off-season experience and extra money.

The predictable result was that he became an absentee father. Arguments over the support and care of his children festered, with the Masons all too aware that as Josh's fame as a ballplayer increased, his relationship with his children became more distant. His one devotion in life was the game, and though he did not reveal any dislike for his children (Josh, Jr., would later tag along as a batboy for the Grays), and while he certainly never abandoned them, the realities of the game he was playing made it all but impossible for him to be a conscientious and responsible parent. And his family suffered for it.

During the remainder of 1930, Josh was a Gray and went where the team went. His long home run against the Lincoln Giants in Yankee Stadium had engraved his name in the minds of opposing players, not to mention the fans. It became a must in Pittsburgh to see the Grays and "Gipson," or Gibson, whatever his name was, hit the ball. He was known as the young slugger "who wrecked the Lincoln Giants." In fact, as hometown sportswriters marveled, "Some of the Lincoln boys still have headaches when they hear his name."

In the fall, he began the first of many years of cross-country exhibition games with white major-league All-Star teams. Though called "All-Star" teams, the big leaguers were generally only a random collection of players appearing along with a top-name star. Dizzy Dean often formed such a team and freely took on black opponents in the off-season. The freewheeling Dean and his brother Paul enjoyed the competition immensely, and even suggested that the style of Negro baseball was in many ways more appealing than the cautious, calculating major-league play.

Though white big leaguers had played the Negro teams for decades, going back to Cap Anson and Ty Cobb's days, there remained a distinctive difference in the way the two approached the game. The Negro game, to most observers, had retained the gambling, rough, unorthodox style of play reminiscent of the days when Cobb flew into second basemen with his spikes high and razor sharp. Black pitchers threw more and different pitches, including those delivered with a ball greased, cut, coarsened, or in some way "doctored." They devised every motion conceivable: sidewinder deliveries, submarine, cross-fire, even countless versions of hesitation pitches. Rules were arbitrary or not at all enforced, the object only to win by getting the batter out.

Besides the pitchers, black ballplayers went about the game in a looser, more unpredictable way, with an abandon that the major leagues had long since lost. The blacks called it "tricky baseball," a term which meant only that rules of baseball strategy or logic didn't always apply and needn't be followed. Bunts, force plays, intentional walks, hit-and-run plays came at unheard-of moments. Pick-off plays used the center fielder, if he was fast enough and quiet enough, slipping behind the runner on second base. Dangerous relays were not uncommon.

Even on the base paths, where runners slid high and hard— Gray outfielder Vic Harris could "undress an infielder, cut the uniform right off his back"—there was no end to the black runner's creativity. James "Cool Papa" Bell, while playing for the St. Louis Stars in 1930, was believed, on more than one occasion, to have gone from first to third without touching second base, running a good three feet inside it so as to cut down on the distance to third. Almost always, he believed, all eyes would be watching the action around the ball in the outfield. And more often than not, especially against off-season white major leaguers, Bell was right.

The white-black match-ups had a peculiar competitiveness to them, even though they were exhibition games. Baseball's formal observers, the white sportswriters around the country, tended to ignore the contests and even suggest that they were played less than seriously. That usually wasn't the case by any means, for the black teams were deadly serious about important ball games, especially games with major leaguers which demanded the best

of them. White teams sensed the challenge and generally felt
that it was bad form and bad politics to get beaten by blacks.

Most of the time, however, the big leaguers had little choice in
the matter. Only the most naive baseball fan attempted to deny
the talent found on the Negro teams, regardless of whether or
not it had been recognized by the majors. Against top black
teams such as the Grays and others, the white major leaguers
had their hands full, and they knew it. All-Star teams headed by
Dizzy Dean played black squads even up, one year losing nine of
sixteen games to a squad with many of the Grays on it.

The black teams won so many games from their white
opponents not only because of the tricky baseball they played but
also because the major leagues by the 1930s had developed a
power-oriented style of baseball. Many fans felt that it was due
to Babe Ruth and his awesome influence on the game. With
such a crowd-pleasing power hitter on a team, a squad was less
apt to make its base runners take chances. It was easier to get on
base, sit tight, and wait for one swing from the mighty Bambino
to clear the bases. Negro baseball, however, even with the
presence of many of its great pre-Gibson sluggers, hadn't
subscribed to such practices and continued to punch and scrape
and jockey its runners and its strategies to the point where the
opposing clubs and fans had to be ready for anything and could
count on nothing.

The competition brought about a certain camaraderie and
respect between white and black players. Perhaps there is no
greater appreciation of talent than that found in the mind of one
similarly blessed, be it the awe of one concert pianist for the
technique of another, a legal mind for the strategy of an
opponent, or a ballplayer who sees the game played with finesse
and style by someone else, regardless of the man's color. But
ballplayers, as previously noted, are not social reformers, and the
appreciation players such as Dizzy Dean, Jimmie Foxx, Grover
Cleveland Alexander, and many others had for the fine black
stars they played did not translate into a combined, energetic

movement to break the color barrier. Their respect went no farther than off-season accolades, an occasional public tribute, or a private kind word.

Dizzy Dean had no qualms about praising black stars to anyone who would listen. Slugger Jimmie Foxx, the Philadelphia Athletic who not only played against blacks in exhibitions and in South American leagues but also associated with them off the field and considered them friends, never muted his regard for black talent.

Yet there were others who were not similarly inclined. The attitude of Cap Anson, the great star of the Chicago White Stockings in the 1880s and 1890s who led a revolt against black ballplayers then in the major leagues, was sustained by Al Simmons, the sensational Philadelphia Athletics outfielder in the 1920s and 1930s. Simmons simply refused to play against blacks. Countless other white players were blatantly hostile, antagonistic, or quietly prejudiced. Some showed it by being unfriendly toward touring blacks no matter what the circumstances. One of the prominent players to do this, in the minds of many black players, was Bob Feller, the superb Cleveland Indians pitcher, who often played against blacks but never had a good word to say about them. That was doubly insulting to black players because they felt that when they played Feller, the crowds turned out to see the stiff competition and how well Feller did against it, and in so doing, paid Feller good money for the challenge.

Attitudes of white major leaguers toward blacks were often casually offensive. In the late 1930s, Jake Powell of the New York Yankees was interviewed on a Chicago radio station and asked what he did in the off-season. "I keep in trim in winter hitting niggers over the head with my club," Powell replied. Later, he attempted to apologize on the air but was refused the opportunity. He even came to the Chicago *Defender* office in Harlem to apologize. Harlem blacks and those throughout the country weren't impressed and attempted to organize a black boycott of Ruppert Beer in protest against Yankee owner Colonel Jake Ruppert.

Josh was to learn the intricacies of professional baseball's racial politics only too well as he continued to play, but in 1930 he was bright-eyed and passive about most of it. He was still flexing his muscles, playing as hard as he could and practicing in between—so much so that he often caught batting practice before games to sharpen his defensive skills.

He lacked confidence in his catching ability, understandably so, for such a complex position demanded the most out of even the veteran receiver. Josh knew he had to learn as much and as fast as he could, for when he first broke in there were half dozen catchers in the Negro leagues who were better, more polished, more intelligent receivers than he was. The best were veteran Biz Mackey of Baltimore, Larry Brown of the Memphis Red Sox, and Tom Young of the Kansas City Monarchs. Frank Duncan, also of the Monarchs, was considered far and away the smartest catcher around, and Homestead's own Buck Ewing could have played on anyone's team. To Josh's credit, he was smart enough and dedicated enough to watch their every move.

That winter he played his first season of baseball in South America, then returned to work in a Pittsburgh department store. No matter what his name was, the Depression was in full force, he was black, and he needed a job in order to live. In early spring 1931, he boarded a bus for Hot Springs, Arkansas, a full-time, first-rate Homestead Gray ready to take on the new season.

As established as the Grays were, with the combined business and baseball minds of Posey and Charlie Walker, the new year again promised to be a precarious one for the team, if not for all of Negro baseball. The Depression was simply too awesome an obstacle. Banks were closing all over the country; in Chicago, a new one closed every two days. As if as an omen for the coming season of Negro ball, Rube Foster, the game's founding father and once most powerful force, died in late December after his long struggle with mental illness. Foster's absence paved the way for the increasing influence of Cum Posey, but that, too, was a dubious proposition, for if the economy became bad enough under the weight of unemployment and bread lines, there might be nothing for Posey to dominate.

In New York, Bill "Bojangles" Robinson bought total control of the Black Yankees, and this marked the first time that the team was owned completely by blacks. At the very least, his new ownership provided Bojangles with unlimited opportunities to entertain the fans with his backward hundred-yard dash. But New York City's economy in 1931 seemed to indicate changes in that city's black community. There was strong feeling among real-estate executives that improvements to buildings and property in Harlem would make that area too valuable for blacks to maintain their hold on it. Nobody knew for sure, and with the Depression at hand, few were willing to guess.

Josh was oblivious of such concerns. He was nineteen and counted on catching regularly for the Grays. After two seasons with the Grays, Buck Ewing decided to quit baseball, a move which actually made things tougher on Josh. Yet once inside Hot Springs' Whittington Park, he took up where he had left off in 1930. Drives flew out of the stadium and landed in the *Courier*'s sports pages in Pittsburgh. He was touted back home as if he had been an established Gray for fifteen years, and as the team moved from Hot Springs down south to play games against the Cuban House of David and other touring teams, his reputation continued to grow.

The Grays had much the same lineup as they had had in 1930. Joining the team was Ted Page, a lanky, fast left-handed outfielder from New York who had played with the team for three weeks in 1930 but left when he found Pittsburgh uncomfortable and gloomy. He came to stay in 1931, however, and was one of the younger Gray players who were naturally attracted to the easygoing, powerful Gibson. Though Page was a contemporary of Josh's, he was not a little bit awed by him and what he could do. They made friends easily, for Josh mingled freely with most ballplayers. He lived with his parents when the Grays were playing around Pittsburgh, but stuck close to Page and some of the other young Grays on the road.

The team traveled around Pittsburgh, into Ohio, New York, and West Virginia during the summer, playing other Negro professional teams and the best of the semipro white teams. Josh's confidence increased with each game, each hit. He connected regularly, hitting for an average but also with an amazing slugging percentage. No official records were kept, as they seldom were for the Grays or any other black team, but it was in this year, when Josh was only nineteen, that he was credited with hitting seventy-five home runs. The figure is difficult to evaluate, however, for no one kept track of how many games the Grays played or what percentage of the games was against top competition. Teammates like Ted Page, Jud Wilson, Jake Stevens, and others never scuttled claims for Josh's power, for they saw him hit every day and hit the ball farther and harder than any other player in the game. His home-run total had many factors involved, one of which was the fact that many fields the Grays played on had no fences, and it wasn't unusual for opposing outfielders to stand 400 feet away when Josh hit, then camp under his long drives.

By the end of the 1931 season, Josh was an established star, the clean-up hitter and mainstay of the Grays' lineup. Cum Posey put him on his unofficial 1931 Negro League All-Star team without hesitation, an honor that meant something because the crusty Posey was not sentimental when it came to gauging his players against the rest of the country's black talent.

With Gibson on Posey's All-Star team were Oscar Charleston of the Grays, first base; Baltimore's Dick Lundy at shortstop; Newt Allen, Kansas City, second base; Jud Wilson, Grays, third base; and Martin Dihigo of Philadelphia's Hilldale, Cool Papa Bell of St. Louis, Deke Mothel of Kansas City, and Mule Suttles of St. Louis in the outfield. Pitchers included the Grays' Joe Williams, Willie Foster, and Teddy Radcliffe; Satchel Paige and Sam Streeter of the Pittsburgh Crawfords; Pud Flournoy of the Baltimore Black Sox; and Charles Beverly of Kansas City.

In Posey's mind, they were the best the Negro leagues had to offer, and with few exceptions and minor additions, the roster stood up well.

But however well any of them played, however many home runs Josh hit, the year was a bad one financially for all of Negro baseball. Even major-league teams were feeling the hard times, and the salaries of the top white stars were decreasing. The future was dubious at best for Negro baseball all over the country unless the Depression eased or the sport received a new influx of cash. Oddly enough, the latter was to be the case in Pittsburgh. For a man there named W. A. "Gus" Greenlee was about to introduce a new era of Negro baseball in that town, one which would outclass any that had come before it. And Greenlee's plans very much included Josh Gibson.

3

That Murderous Bat

Even in a day without television, so many people saw him hit a baseball. Their descriptions do not vary much, only the details: the number of home runs, or the length of the drives, which fence each one cleared. The years have sweetened the memories, no doubt, the mixture of legend and myth growing stronger every day. Only the vision of how he did it, how he stood in the batter's box, gripped the bat, and connected with a fastball seems to have been etched in the minds of the witnesses.

One of the common criticisms of Negro baseball in the days of the color barrier was that it lacked technique. Not style, mind you, but textbook form for hitting, pitching, and fielding. It was true, perhaps, but laughably appropriate to how well the black ballplayers performed. So many of them were never taught the game by a competent coach. They learned it in a sandlot or by watching the older players, and they picked up bad habits and kept them until someone took the time to show them differently. Henry Aaron batted cross-handed for years until a coach told him about it. He hit some ferocious home runs that way, but he changed and found he could hit even more. Roy Campanella stepped back with his right foot just before swinging, a flaw called "stepping in the bucket," and even though he was coached on it he never really licked the tendency, but it never kept him from being one of the hardest-hitting catchers in the major leagues. Hundreds of other black players had "unacceptable" traits as hitters and fielders, from nervously twitching the bat before each pitch to catching flies by cupping their mitts at their belts, as Willie Mays so often did. But such things never really bothered anyone in the Negro leagues as long as a man could get the job done. Form was something the major leaguers could worry about, something white kids could spend hours fussing over. Blacks were too busy playing the game to pay much attention to it.

Oddly enough, Josh as a hitter was a model of textbook form. Nobody had ever taught it to him, and nobody ever tampered with it. His only defect was his stance: an upright, flat-footed posture, somewhat rigid, especially because he didn't stride much or bend his back and knees. Yet it didn't matter when he played for the Crawford Giants or during his first years with the Grays because he had such a tremendous eye, lightning reflexes, and an ability to get the bat on the ball.

It wasn't long, however, before he had perfected his batting style to the point where it became flawless. Josh's power came almost completely from strength above his waist: arms, shoulders, and back muscles so awesome that he didn't need the coiled power of his legs or the whiplike action of his wrists. With his upper-body power, he could thrash a ball with a motion much like that of beating a rug. He stood flat-footed, his heavy bat gripped down to the end and held high above his right shoulder, his feet spread fairly wide apart, and with the pitch he strode only slightly—some say about four inches, some say not at all, but simply raised his foot and put it down in the same spot when the pitch came.

Such a batting stride is in drastic contrast to so many power hitters such as Babe Ruth or Mickey Mantle, who took a long, perhaps twelve- to eighteen-inch stride and waded into a pitch with the commitment of the total body. Depending on the amount of talent involved, such a stride usually meant that a power hitter found himself off-balance when fooled by a pitch, or, when he connected, that his entire body met the ball and walloped it. Josh did no such thing. His short stride and massive strength seldom put him off-balance, seldom found him over-committed or unable to compensate when fooled by a pitch or when he had to reach for it. It also gave him a short swing, a limited arc of the bat that was concentrated in a smaller area than the wide, twisting, blustering swing of a Ruth or Mantle. Take many of the great long-ball hitters, from Ruth, Jimmie Foxx, and Mel Ott, to Willie Mays, Mantle, Willie McCovey, and Willie Stargell, and you see monstrous roundhouse swings that are ferocious and powerful and wonderful to watch when they connect and perhaps even more delightful when they miss. But with Josh (and some other power hitters, like Henry Aaron, Ernie Banks, and, to some extent, Roger Maris), the swing was smaller, more condensed, more concentrated. The final result was just as productive as Ruth-style swings, but not nearly so picturesque. Josh was a treasure to watch when he connected, but not a spectacle when he struck out.

Josh patterned his style after Lou Gehrig of the Yankees, a player Josh felt was more polished in more techniques than any player at the time. When the Grays were in the vicinity of the Yankees during Gehrig's day, Josh made every effort to see him, something made more possible after 1930 when the Grays had some free afternoons before playing night games. He also greatly admired Jimmie Foxx, not only because Foxx was right-handed as Josh was, but also because the slugger was so friendly to blacks during the off-season. Foxx also was built much like Josh—Foxx weighed 195 and stood six feet tall—and was the premier home-run hitter in the majors in the 1930s when Ruth slowed down and finally retired. Almost from the beginning of Josh's pro career, he rolled up the short sleeves of his uniform, a move which showed off his massive biceps and which mimicked Foxx.

Josh's overwhelming strength at the plate came from his batting eye and his bat control. Throughout his career he was always an "average" hitter, meaning that he hit for a high average as well as for home runs. Part of that success was due to his speed, but most of it was due to the fact that he hit the ball where it was pitched, and hit it hard. Most who played with Josh claim nobody hit the ball as *hard* as he did—liners that tore the gloves off infielders, line drives that cracked against fences. His small stride made him a good curveball and change-up hitter. Josh quickly learned, according to teammate Buck Leonard, to bend his back when he went after curves, a technique essential to hitting the pitch, and had little trouble with them or other off-speed pitches. But he also hit pitches thrown all over the strike zone, a necessity in Negro leagues because umpires tended to call strikes on pitches ranging anywhere between the top of the shoulders and the knees. Major-league umpires through the years have restricted the strike zone to an area between the armpits and the top of the kneecaps.

Apart from his formidable strength and his near-perfect form, Josh had the awesome quality of courage that all good hitters must have if they are to survive. No one thing comes more into play in the battle between pitcher and hitter. It is a natural tendency for a batter to step away from something thrown at him, not stride into it. On the lowest levels of baseball, from Little Leaguers to semiprofessionals, it is not uncommon to see the majority of hitters stepping away from the ball, pulling the lead leg, the body, and the head away from the pitch for no other reason than the fact that a baseball is hard as a rock, is thrown at anywhere from forty to ninety miles an hour, and tends to hurt and hurt badly when it hits a bone. The step-away tendency is an understandable one, but close to poison for any aspiring hitter.

A pro is able to stride into the ball time after time, even after he has been dusted back or hit in the neck, and face off the pitcher with a bat that covers all parts of the strike zone. Josh, from the beginning of his career, could do it without flinching. When he became a premier slugger, he was thrown at more and more, for Negro leagues were freewheeling in every way, including the beanball, which was looked upon not as impolite

or dirty but as a strategic weapon to be used against hitters like
Josh who dug in and ruined you. Josh was thrown at and
beaned often, but it never fazed him. Often, with two strikes and
no balls as a count, he knew he was going to get a fastball sailing
at his ear. He often bent down and picked up a handful of dirt
and looked back at the pitcher as if to say that he knew what was
coming and he'd been there before. Then the dustback pitch
came, and Josh either hit the dirt or was hit in the head. But he
got back up and hit as he always had, giving no pitcher a break,
never showing a crack in the courage that he needed to hit the
ball. To him and most other hitters in the league, it wasn't
heroic, just something a good hitter had to do to stay on top. Josh
stayed.

His home runs were most often long drives, deep, not necessarily high but often so; or quick, smashing blows that flew off
the bat and rushed out of the stadium. They were, in every sense
of the word, "Ruthian," for Babe's considerable strength made
so many of his home runs tape-measure clouts. Yet to so many
who saw the way Josh hit them day in and day out, they were
"Gibsonian," with a power and velocity equal to anything Ruth
ever hit. The most memorable were to dead center field, a mark
of perfect contact between bat and ball at the precisely perfect
instant. Yet he pulled as many to left, and nailed others into the
right-field stands. Few people remember Josh's home runs as
being restricted to any one field, and mention that they were
similar only in the way they disappeared.

The stories go on and on. He hit so many, and so many saw
them go. There are the tales about Josh hitting one out of sight
on one afternoon only to have it reappear out of the sky the next
day. Of course, the umpire said, "Yer out! Yesterday, in
Pittsburgh!" And there are the less apocryphal stories of games
being stopped in mid-inning so the home team could measure the
blow. The mayor of Monessen, Pennsylvania, did it one day,
arriving at a distance of 512 feet.

The most engaging stories are from teammates or opponents

who remember what it was like to play with him each day, and who saw the best of the Negro leagues and the white leagues try to outfox him or fake him out, fool him or overpower him.

Jack Marshall, who played most of his career with Chicago's Negro teams but who hooked on with Josh during the off-season or south of the border, remembers not a home run but a line-drive single Josh hit in York, Pennsylvania, one day. It shot off his bat at shortstop Willie Wells, one of the Negro leagues' greatest shortstops, but Wells couldn't do anything with it. The ball hit Wells's glove so hard that it split the skin on his left hand. Wells, like most fielders of the era who wore compact, short-fingered gloves, caught most infield hits in the pocket of the glove and built up a tough, callused palm. But Josh's drive went through his glove and, said Marshall, "split the web of skin between his thumb and his first finger right apart."

Marshall also vividly remembers one of Josh's "quick" drives, one hit in Comiskey Park in Chicago. Comiskey was a major-league stadium with long fences, and its center-field wall was 435 feet from home plate. On it, about 8 feet off the ground, were loudspeakers facing toward the field and about 20 inches in diameter. Josh hit a drive to straightaway center that to Marshall never seemed to rise, staying instead on a straight line like a frozen rope. It struck a loudspeaker dead center and stuck in it like an apple. The game was stopped while a groundskeeper pried it free.

Jimmie Crutchfield played alongside Josh for five years and against him for many more, and he can think of countless times that Josh left everyone in the stands wide-eyed. Crutchfield remembers a game against the Nashville Elite Giants which was played in front of a big crowd, including a complete minor-league team who made the game just to see Josh perform. The Elite Giants' manager was Candy Jim Taylor, who said before the game that he know how to pitch Josh. Taylor insisted that Josh could not hit a sidewinder, a pitch fired from the third-base side of the mound. During a crucial time in the game, with

Josh's team behind, Cool Papa Bell doubled, Crutchfield followed with a single, and Josh came up representing the go-ahead run. Taylor quickly stopped the game and went out to instruct his pitcher, Andrew Porter, to throw nothing but sidewinders. According to Crutchfield, Josh dug in at the plate and waited for his pitch. When he got it, a sidewinder coming at him and snaking for the outside of the plate, Josh stroked it. "I can see it now," said Jimmie. "It just went out of the park like the wind."

It seemed Josh hit best against the best, against tough Negro-league pitchers who faced him down and made him hit what they had. His tremendous home run in Yankee Stadium against the Lincoln Giants in September 1930, only months after he had joined the Grays at age eighteen, came during the heat of a tough series against Cornelius "Connie" Rector, one of the best Negro-league pitchers of the time. Cum Posey considered it one of the greatest hits of Josh's career, and one which came under enormous pressure.

Yankee Stadium, "the House That Ruth Built," brought out the best in Josh whenever he set foot inside the park. Against the New York Black Yankees (oddly enough, one of Negro baseball's weaker franchises through the years, even though it potentially had one of the biggest followings), Josh hit three homers one Sunday afternoon in the early 1930s. One of them, as Black Yankee shortstop Bill Yancey remembers, was another of Josh's unforgettable "quick" home runs. "He walloped three that day and one of them was the quickest home run I ever saw. It was out of the park before the outfielders could turn their heads to watch it. It landed behind the Yankee Stadium bullpen, some five hundred feet away. He didn't loft it, he shot it out of there."

Another of his Yankee Stadium clouts went to right field, landing in Tier 26. By all accounts, that was six tiers farther than one hit by Jimmie Foxx, a drive at that time considered the longest ever hit in those seats.

Other major-league parks were comparably assaulted. Cum Posey considered a Gibson home run to straightaway center field in Pittsburgh's Forbes Field as the longest ever hit there. Posey insisted that only Josh and John Beckwith, an awesome power hitter with a variety of teams in the 1920s, had ever popped one over that fence. One of Josh's blasts over the right-field wall in Cincinnati's Crosley Field was considered one of the longest ever hit there, and similarly branded was a home run in Cleveland's Municipal Stadium.

In Washington's Griffith Stadium, a ball park in which Josh played many games later in his career, his home-run totals rivaled those of the entire major-league Washington Senator squad. That stadium was lined with twenty-foot-high walls covered with advertising. Once Josh hit a line drive against the right-field fence which slammed into a hot-dog sign, knocking paint and dust everywhere. A fan quickly yelled, "B'gosh! Josh knocked the mustard off that dog!"

Less remembered are the countless home runs Josh hit in small-town ball parks against semipro teams. He hit four homers in four at bats one day in Zanesville, Ohio. He hit three straight in Fairmont, West Virginia. And there was the mayor of Monessen, Pennsylvania, with his tape measure. That was an event like one on an afternoon in San Juan, Puerto Rico. That day Josh was playing in a stadium located next to a prison. He hit one over two fences—the ball park's and the prison's— narrowly missing inmates standing 525 feet away from home plate.

It was home runs like those, most of them unrecorded and untotaled, which comprised much of Josh's record. Many observers believed the total to be more than a thousand in all, a believable count in view of the number of games Josh played, but one impossible to verify.

Nothing sullies the remembrance of Josh's golden moments as witnessed by fellow Negro-league performers. Buck Leonard remembers a game against Leon Day and the Newark Eagles in which the Grays were behind, 2-1. When a runner got on first, Leonard sacrificed him to second, one of the few times the hard-hitting Leonard ever bunted. Josh could tie the game with a single, so Day bore down on him. He got two strikes past Josh and prepared to set him up for a third. Again, Josh was the kind of hitter, as his teammates insist to this day, who never worried about two strikes on him. He didn't shorten up or widen his stance. He believed he could hit anything in any situation, and simply had the confidence he would. Day wound up and threw a tough two-strike pitch, a fast curveball on the outside of the plate, and Josh nailed it over the scoreboard in center field. It was a blast which not only broke up the ball game but which had people slapping their foreheads in disbelief. "He was that kind of power hitter," Leonard said. "Nobody knows how far that ball went that day."

Or the time Jack Marshall saw him commit himself too soon and almost strike out on a sucker pitch. Almost. For as Marshall remembers it, Sonny Cornelius was pitching for the American Giants against the Grays at Victory Field in Indianapolis, Indiana. Cornelius threw Josh a good slow curve and fooled him completely. Josh took his short stride, shifted his weight as much as he ever did, and began his swing. He brought his left arm across his body, but halted the motion at the sight of Cornelius's tantalizing slow curve, let go of the bat with his left hand, and with only his right hand gripping the handle, swatted at the ball as if he were going after a horsefly. The drive carried 375 feet and out of the park. Josh circled the bases, unable to contain a smile; Sonny Cornelius shook his head.

Even with such power, such amazing home runs, Josh was seldom seen hotdogging when he circled the bases. His talent and power were natural to him, and he din't feel the need to rub it into opposing players. When he was just breaking in, he occasionally razzed opposing pitchers as he circled the bases, but he did it competitively, not to mock or taunt them. He might have done more of it if it had been in him, but Gibson's personality right from the start was withdrawn and modest in most respects. He saw the leverage that some players got out of being showboats and crowd-pleasers, and he often tried to join in. But it wasn't really a natural facility. He was an attraction with a bat in his hands and he knew that. If the rest did not come, he would not force it.

He had his problems hitting on occasion, like everybody else. He fell into slumps, he struck out, and he had pitchers he could not get to. Teddy "Big Florida" Trent of the American Giants was one. Trent threw a good slider and a variety of curves, described by one teammate as "a long one, a short one, and a shorter one," all of which made him tough on Josh. Larry Brown, whose job as one of the fine catchers of black baseball was to help pitchers outwit Josh, said that Josh was "perhaps the best natural hitter and hardest slugger in Negro baseball." Brown said that he could not find Josh's weakness and that so many times after a particular pitcher had struck out Gibson and was convinced he could handle him, "Josh came back and knocked the pitch out of the park."

Chet Brewer, the fine Chicago American Giant and Kansas City Monarch hurler, had his moments against Josh. Yet Brewer was never convinced of his success and maintained that Josh hit so well because he had such amazing coordination and control at the plate. "He could hit any pitch to any field. The only way to pitch to him was to throw the ball low and behind him."

Yet the hardest on Josh, as he was on almost every other hitter in baseball, was the gangling Satchel Paige. Josh's hits against Paige were "few and far between," by his own admission, and he never effortlessly touched Satchel for homers. Paige, for his part, played many years alongside Gibson. When he opposed Josh, he said he had as difficult a time as anyone. "You look for his weakness and while you lookin' for it he liable to hit forty-five home runs," Satchel said.

The stories are repeated into the night; the blasts longer, more awesome, more impossible. Paige claims Josh hit one off the scoreboard clock in Wrigley Field, a drive which would have had to have been heading for a distance of 700 feet. It is most unlikely that Gibson ever came close, for the clock stands 100 feet up and once was barely reached by Sam Snead and a three-iron.

But such tales are the stuff of legends, and they grow taller as the years pass.

One claim for Josh's power, however, outdoes them all. Yankee Stadium is so massive, with its outfield bleachers built so far and high from home plate, that no man, including Babe Ruth, ever hit one completely out of the stadium. Yet Josh walloped one there that came close, so close that through the years legend has put it completely out of the park. It just wasn't so, however.

In the years since their demise, because of the lack of data and official information recorded during the era, the Negro leagues and the feats of individual players have been nurtured and expanded by those articulate enough to do so. Josh's Yankee Stadium blast is the perfect example. Jack Marshall of the Chicago American Giants has been quoted over and over again (most notably and, unfortunately, most authoritatively, in Robert Peterson's *Only the Ball Was White*) to the extent that he was in Yankee Stadium in July 1934, and saw Josh hit one out of the park. Marshall said he and the Giants had played the first game of a four-team doubleheader one Sunday and were standing in the aisles about to leave for a game in Hightstown, New Jersey. He watched as the Pittsburgh Crawfords and Josh played the Philadelphia Stars. "Josh hit one out in left center, by the bullpen out there and over the triple deck. I saw it," Marshall was quoted. And so it was written, and so it has been passed along from fan to fan, and even among Josh's former teammates.

Judy Johnson phrases it delicately by saying Josh hit the only ball "I ever read of" which went out of Yankee Stadium. Judy was playing third base for the Crawfords in that 1934 game, and he would have seen and no doubt remembered such a Gibson homer. Cool Papa Bell was the Crawford center fielder and he doesn't remember such a clout. Bell says also that he only "heard" of Josh doing it but that it happened when Bell wasn't playing with him, a point which would rule out the 1934 game.

In fact, the four teams mentioned by Marshall played a Yankee Stadium doubleheader only twice in the 1934 season. In one, the American Giants and the Black Yankees played the second game and would not have been standing in aisles watching the Crawfords and Stars finish out the day. In the Crawford game of that doubleheader, Slim Jones pitched for the Stars and was beaten, 3-1. No home runs were hit; Josh got a single in four at bats.

In the doubleheader Marshall was probably referring to, the Stars and the Crawfords did play the second game and Slim Jones again pitched. But the game was called after nine innings because of darkness, with the score tied at 1-1. Again, no home runs were hit. Josh went 0-4.

With all due respect to Jack Marshall and his memory, there exists no record and no written account of an out-of-the-park homer in Yankee Stadium. Through the years nobody but Marshall claimed to have seen such a Gibson hit. That covers a period when sportswriters, including the punctilious Cum Posey, lingered for paragraphs over specific base hits and home runs. Josh himself never spoke of such a hit. In 1943, when he wrote of his career highlights in the Pittsburgh *Courier*, he mentioned the 1930 home run against the Lincoln Giants, and he cited the blast that stopped the game in Monessen, Pennsylvania. The latter was the longest of his career, he added.

But no Yankee Stadium clout. In a day when he was constantly being compared to Babe Ruth, it seems improbable that he would not have capitalized on a feat that would have put him in at least one category directly superior to Ruth.

He never did because it never happened.

Though Josh was born to be a catcher—his build and his toughness the prime requisites for the position—he was not an instant one. Catching is a complex, multifaceted job that takes raw physical strength to endure the countless foul tips to the fingers, legs, and crotch, the swinging bats on the side of the head, the wild pitches in the stomach, the collisions with base runners, and the constant squatting and bending of the knees to receive the pitch, retrieve it, and return it. Then it takes brains to guide a pitcher, to call his pitches, place the glove, outmaneuver the batter, and cajole the umpire. And on top of all that, the catcher is supposed to anchor a team up the middle, keep his infielders aware and instruct them on the situation at hand, and supply an arsenal of chatter and encouragement lest everyone fall asleep. If a runner strays from the bases, the catcher should pick him off, and he should nail any and all base stealers with a frozen rope of a peg that should come from his ear, rise no higher than four feet off the ground, and hiss into his fielder's glove just inches above the bag. All catchers, Josh included, through all the eras of the game, have had to do such things for better or worse. And none of them, including Josh, found it very easy.

Through the years, especially when he wasn't hitting shots into the third deck and making fans forget about everything else, Josh was held in varying esteem as a catcher. He was once described as "a weak member in that department." Plays such as a wild pick-off throw in the 1933 All-Star game didn't help much, but he made up for such lapses. In the 1934 All-Star game, he cut down Sammy Bankhead with a brilliant peg as Bankhead attempted to steal second base.

In his early seasons with the Grays and the Crawfords, Josh impressed with his speed—he was quick for a big man and possessed good hands despite the fact that the catcher's glove of his time was a fat, round saucer of leather with a molded pocket no bigger than the ball (many modern-day catcher's mitts are shaped like oblong baskets, much like first baseman's gloves, and can be used to snag the ball instead of catching it square in the pocket)—and his hustle, and unflagging enthusiasm and chatter no matter how lopsided the score or how many games he had already caught that day.

But Josh's greatest asset as a catcher was his durability. He was seldom injured severely enough to keep him out of action for any length of time. In fact, until the last few years of his career, only the layoff due to an appendectomy in 1932 kept him sidelined for more than a day or two. And through those years, playing with the Grays, Crawfords, All-Star teams, and clubs south of the border, he was behind the plate taking the beating that that position gives.

Occasionally he was put in left field in order to keep his bat in the lineup, but he never stayed there long. In 1933, he was listed at third base, and sometimes he dallied at strange positions against weak sandlot teams. But he remained a catcher. If he wasn't photographed with a bat in his hand, he posed in his gear, his hat turned backward and accentuating his wide, flat forehead, the bulky chest protector with its crotch flap, his immense forearms and the chunky glove hanging on his hip, the armorlike shin guards over his legs. As a hitter stopping in midswing for a photographer, he often flashed a toothy grin; as a catcher he posed full front with his legs apart, or crouched with his right hand clenched and stared impassively, silently communicating the fact that the sweat and grimy dust and whistling foul tips of a catcher's life were unglamorous and unamusing.

Those who played with him considered him a good catcher; not a great one, not the best one, but a solid receiver. Judy Johnson, who played with Josh from the day Josh relieved Buck Ewing, considered him just that way. "He was not a Campanella, but he could run, had a good arm, and he did the job," Judy said.

Yet Roy Campanella, who was coming into the leagues as a rookie when Josh was in the prime of his career, considered Josh his idol and felt that, as a catcher, "I couldn't carry Josh's

glove. Anything I could do, Josh could do better." That may be a
bit of largesse from one pro to another, and Campanella through
the years tempered his praise for Josh's catching prowess.

Campanella spoke from a solid point of reference, however,
for he was tutored by one of the best catchers who ever lived. Biz
Mackey of the Baltimore Elite Giants was the pro Josh looked
to as a catcher when he broke in in 1930, and who was still
playing when Campanella came up in 1937. The grizzled
Mackey caught for more than thirty years, until he was past
fifty, and no man in Negro baseball surpassed his ability to
handle the position. He was brilliant defensively and superb at
handling pitchers, and also, incidentally, had a right hand that
best showed the rigors of the position. Mackey's throwing hand
was broken a dozen times in his career, every finger was at one
time mashed, twisted, sprained, or fractured to the point where
the fist became a mangled cluster of bumps and knobs. Still,
Mackey did the job, and nothing Josh ever did as a catcher cut
into Biz's sterling reputation. And Campanella, as Mackey's
protégé first in the Negro leagues then as a Brooklyn Dodger,
sustained it.

Josh did have a powerful, accurate arm. In an informal
pregame track meet among the Crawfords in 1932, he won the
long-distance toss. Behind the plate he was not easy to run
against and frequently picked runners off third base in a pre-
arranged play with Judy Johnson. He had what is called a short
throw, something vital to a catcher because he cannot afford to
take much time to wind up and release his peg. Josh's came from
behind his ear as he was still in his crouch. Again, it was a
much-practiced copy of the textbook catcher's toss, something
Josh worked on over and over until he had mastered it.

As a Crawford, Josh was generally considered to be still
developing as a catcher, picking up savvy, dealing with pitchers,
building confidence to throw, but he never became known for
any significant weaknesses. As the years passed, particularly
when he rejoined the Grays, he did the job superbly day after

day. When Buck Leonard joined the team, he found he was learning a lot from Josh. The two of them sat in the dugout watching opposing pitchers, and Josh pointed out peculiar quirks and habits in a pitcher's motion which he believed could be taken advantage of. By then he was a seasoned pro, an established, respected catcher.

Always he demonstrated his remarkable strength. He could catch anything a pitcher threw at him, block any wild pitch with fearless ease, and bounce back after a collision or an injury. A mark of his strength was found in the way that he recovered from a recurring problem with his shoulder. On a number of occasions the shoulder would pop out of joint and hang immobile. It was painful and bothersome, but something that Josh had endured since his childhood days. Harry Kincannon, who had played ball with Josh from sandlot days, was usually the one to run on the field and help jerk the shoulder back in place. And Josh, after a few practice throws and grimaces, continued on with the game.

It wasn't quite as easy with foul pop flies. Josh often had trouble following and catching them, and it was the one weakness his teammates most remember. He had difficulty getting his bearings once he flipped off his mask and went after the fly, even to the point of getting dizzy as he looked upward and attempted to track the ball. First basemen, especially Buck Leonard, tried to help out and catch fouls for him. That wasn't always possible, and Josh's disorientation often permitted the ball to drop out of his reach. Few knew it at the time, but the problem was a foreshadowing of things to come, a physical condition that even one so strong and gutsy as he was would be unable to overcome.

Still, Josh's weaknesses were only relative ones, and are mentioned in light of his overall magnificent talents. With his power, his eye, his tremendous appeal as a power hitter, he would have satisfied any team if he had been able only to stand behind the plate and let pitches bounce off him. Instead, Josh was a smooth, efficient, reliable catcher who apologized to no one for his defensive skills. Had his, and most anyone else's, defensive talents not paled in comparison with his hitting ability, his catching would not be even casually scrutinized.

4

The Craws

DO YOU CONSIDER AMOS 'N' ANDY A REFLECTION ON YOUR RACE? ARE YOU AMOS OR ARE YOU ANDY? DO YOU KNOW ANY OTHER RACE OF PEOPLE WHO WOULD ALLOW THEMSELVES TO BE SO EXPLOITED? So began the campaign in 1931 against one of the most popular radio programs of the day. "Amos 'n' Andy" was the voice of black people to millions of Americans who sat in front of their radios and howled with laughter. Yet the voices, the characters, and the creative perspectives behind the show were those of two white men, Charles Correll and Freeman Gosden, and while the program was at times outrageously funny, most of the humor came at the expense of the image of black people.

Blacks, for the most part, were upset about the show, but their protestations fell against overwhelming mass-audience approval and a radio network flushed with the good times of a winner. When individual appeals and editorials failed, black newspapers began petition drives. The Pittsburgh *Courier* ran the bold headline week after week: WANTED! ONE MILLION SIGNERS. A NATIONWIDE PROTEST AGAINST AMOS 'N' ANDY. It went on to rail against what it called "radio propaganda." For anyone listening to the program, the *Courier* said, would see all Negro women portrayed as prostitutes, "lawyers as rogues and shysters," and blacks in general as inarticulate, stupid, superstitious, and lazy.

The *Courier* and other papers had no difficulty getting petition signers, but the movement could not slow the success of the show. It ran nonstop for years, with such amazing popular-

56

ity that department stores noticed a definite slack in business when the program was on. The radio program finally went off the air in 1946, yet the series was re-created for television in 1966. By then civil rights had progressed to the point where protests from blacks brought a quick end to the series.

"Amos 'n' Andy" was but a small, if blatant, example of the country's overall racial attitudes. Segregation was the law of the land in the South, discrimination the accepted practice in the North. It was not uncommon for large theaters in cities like Chicago and New York to prohibit black patronage, called "Jim Crowing." When it was done, it was assailed by black leaders and journalists, but few establishments altered their policies.

Yet the indignities of a racist radio program and Jim Crow laws were injustices secondary to a general denial of equal opportunity, especially in jobs. The Chicago *Defender* pleaded for employment opportunities in the face of an economic depression that in the 1930s meant hard times for whites and downright horrible times for blacks. In each issue, the *Defender* listed nine demands:

1. Opening of trades and trade unions to blacks.
2. Representation in President's Cabinet.
3. Engineer and firemen on all railroads.
4. Representation on police forces.
5. Government schools open to Americans in preference to foreigners.
6. Conductors on all railroads.
7. Motormen and conductors on surface lines (streetcars).
8. Federal legislation to abolish lynching.
9. Full enfranchisement for all citizens.

Such issues were life-and-death concerns for black people as far as *Defender* publisher Robert C. Abbott was concerned. Though he gave ample space in his paper to sports news, Abbott considered sports and such things as baseball as trivial interests. He said he personnally had never attended a major-league game and wouldn't as long as blacks were barred. He had made that vow thirty years earlier, he said, when Charlie Grant was dropped from the Baltimore Orioles. Grant was the victim of an attempt in 1901 by John McGraw, then manager of the Orioles, to pass a black man off as an Indian. A member of the Columbia Giants, a Negro team in Chicago, Grant was signed by McGraw, then given the name Charlie Tokohama. McGraw was challenged by other owners and eventually lost his nerve and dropped Grant from the Orioles. That was enough for Abbott, who said he had been on his way to a ball park when he read of Grant's fate and had turned around and gone to the movies instead.

But the crusading *Defender* publisher wasn't about to deny his readers coverage of baseball, one of the few events in 1932 that diverted minds from the Depression. It cost thirty-five cents to get into the best seats at a Negro-league game, twenty-five cents for grandstand and bleacher tickets, a bargain to most any pocketbook. When the survival of the sport came into question, as it did in early 1932 and so many other years, Abbott and the *Defender* followed the story closely. Black baseball owners assembled that winter uncertain whether they could last the season, or if anything resembling the operation Rube Foster had organized in the 1920s would come again.

William A. "Gus" Greenlee wasn't at those meetings, nor was he looked upon as one of the known quantities of Negro baseball by such as Cum Posey. Yet by late summer of 1931, Greenlee had already begun to make his name in the game, and it would prove to be bigger, flashier, and more memorable than any owner's since Rube Foster.

Greenlee had come to Pittsburgh in 1920 from Marion, North Carolina, after serving overseas in World War I. After a few years he put his name behind the Crawford Grille on Wylie Avenue, but almost everyone in Pittsburgh's black community knew the husky, bejowled, cigar-smoking Greenlee, whom they called "Big Red," as one of the slickest numbers kings around. The Grille was just one of the ways he spread his money around, and it provided a central location for his numbers runners and his games. With money came political power on the North Side, but even that was not as desirable to him as was control of a top-rank baseball team. Like most of Greenlee's ventures, he decided to build it from the bottom up.

He started in 1931 by taking over the Crawford Giants, the same sandlot team Josh had played for for three years before he joined the Grays. The Giants were well-known and well-liked on the North Side, but that popularity was nothing compared to what was to come. In the late summer of 1931, Greenlee bought the contract of Leroy "Satchel" Paige from the disbanding Cleveland Cubs for $250, a price far above what the rest of the Giants were making and a forecast of the money Greenlee was prepared to offer for top players.

Greenlee wasn't about to chip his way into organized Negro baseball. He decided to seed his own franchise first by building a complete stadium complex for his team. It was called Greenlee Field (Gus never left any doubt as to who was in charge) and he built it on Bedford Avenue with $100,000 of his own money. He stated for the record that increased black attendance at games in Forbes Field represented a need for a ball park closer to the black community. That was only part of his thinking, for Greenlee really meant that he wouldn't use a white man's field if he didn't have to.

While the Crawford Giants as a sandlot team played at Ammon Field and only occasionally used Forbes Field, the Homestead Grays had played there for years. And though they paid healthy fees for its use, they were never really welcomed there. The Pittsburgh Pirate management did not allow the Grays or other black teams to use the locker rooms. Black teams had to dress and shower in the local YMCA facilities, a drive across town from Forbes. With Greenlee Field, a park with major-league proportions although it seated only 6,000, Gus afforded black players first-class accommodations. Locked shower rooms would no longer be a problem or an indignity.

In early 1932, Greenlee stocked his roster by signing the best talent he could get his hands on. His wasn't a baseball mind, but he did know talent and which team in Negro baseball had most of it. That meant the Homestead Grays. In a matter of weeks in 1932, Greenlee went after the cream of the Gray starting lineup, intent on making them members of Gus Greenlee's Pittsburgh Crawfords. The Craws.

He started by signing veteran Oscar Charleston as playing manager. He added third baseman Judy Johnson and outfielder Ted Page. He already had Satchel Paige and another tough Pittsburgh pitcher, Sam Streeter. He then looked to the premier Pittsburgh slugger, young Josh Gibson.

By February 1932, Greenlee's park was almost finished. That same month he offered Gibson a contract. Josh had just turned twenty-one and he knew nothing about business. But he did know that he was dealing with two of the most aggressive and powerful men in Negro baseball. Cum Posey was not about to watch himself be overshadowed in baseball matters in Pittsburgh or anywhere else. He had dominated the winter owners' meetings of the Negro National League, sustaining his reputation as being the "Moses" of black baseball in the absence of Rube Foster. Yet in head-on-head business dealings with Gus Greenlee, Posey's stature counted for little.

Posey offered Josh a contract the night before Greenlee came with one. Josh signed Posey's contract, and in Posey's mind that was the end of things for the 1932 season. But Josh, perhaps on the advice of Roy Williams, a close friend and pitcher who had just signed with the Crawfords, also signed Greenlee's contract. Though it was denied that money was the issue, Greenlee's offer was slightly better than Posey's. Greenlee also had the pull of a dynamic new team, a new ball field, and an organization which promised to be one of the best in Negro baseball.

Posey vehemently registered his protest, something he could

do to owners and fans alike via a column he wrote for the *Courier* entitled "Posey's Paragraphs," which was reprinted in most Negro newspapers. In it, Posey said that Josh had asked for a Gray contract but was "induced" to sign with the Crawfords. "As Gibson is very young, he is easily advised," Posey wrote, and added that Josh had been "poorly advised." The solution was simple to Posey, however, for contracts were binding once signed by stars even as big as Gibson, the veteran owner insisted.

Posey then proclaimed that if Gibson did not play with the Grays in 1932, "he will not play in Pittsburgh. Today, baseball is a business. It is time an example was made of a few players who have no respect for their signed obligations but will jump to any club for a few dollars more."

It sounded impressive, but Posey lacked the muscle to back it up. Greenlee kept his promises to Josh and the other Crawfords, the new stadium was completed, and the prospects for his Pittsburgh Crawfords in 1932 looked excellent. Josh was convinced that the Crawfords were the way to go and decided to stay with the team. The fact that the tough, competent Oscar Charleston was going to manage the Craws and that Josh's early mentor, Judy Johnson, was going to play third base was an overwhelming attraction.

Posey's threats notwithstanding, the prospect of being blackballed by the Negro leagues, or even penalized for jumping a contract, was remote and had been so ever since the leagues had begun. Team owners didn't have the organization or the power to effectively control players, and the leagues didn't have the binding strength to keep players and owners alike in line. Players were repeatedly jumping contracts or signing with two teams simultaneously, a situation which could have been worked to their good fortune if there had been any money to be made in Negro baseball. More often than not, the highest salary offer, even from a wallet like Greenlee's, was a pittance.

On February 18, Josh boarded a bus headed for Hot Springs,

Arkansas, and spring training with the Crawfords. Posey lost considerable face back in Pittsburgh for not keeping his catcher. Yet being the baseball politician that he was, Posey decided to let things ride and look after his Grays. He did not hesitate, however, to level a few shots at Greenlee in his sports-page columns. He said in print that Greenlee was nothing but a numbers man, running his gambling out of the same building that housed the West Penn News Service, a black news syndicate. It was West Penn, wrote Posey, that was responsible for a series of articles charging Posey with attempting to dominate organized Negro baseball.

Posey went on to claim that John L. Clark, the author of the West Penn releases, had been a reporter for the Pittsburgh *American,* a black newspaper, but was hired away from the paper by Greenlee to keep him from continuing a series on the city's numbers rackets. Greenlee, according to Posey, told associates that "Clark had to be put someplace to keep his mouth shut." Posey then said that it was lamentable that Clark had compromised himself and that he was now helping Greenlee further the notion that Posey was trying to exercise control over the Crawfords by trying to force them into organized Negro ball.

"The real truth," wrote Posey, "is that in 1931 when the Crawfords were floundering around looking for games, I lent them the services of my brother Seward to book games for them."

The spat between the two owners did little but make for good off-season reading for *Courier* buyers. (It was also the start of a nasty feud between Posey and Clark which lasted for years.) Posey later insisted there was no "warfare" between the Grays and the Craws and that each team would do the best they could in the coming year. Privately, he resented Greenlee and considered him a racketeer instead of a baseball man. But he was not to deny the financial input Gus would give to Pittsburgh baseball. Posey's Grays were still very much a part of that.

Greenlee didn't stick around to continue the battle. In late

February he got delivery on a brand-new twenty-two-passenger Mack bus, a long-nosed beauty that cost him $10,000 and had his name painted on the side. With its 6-cylinder, 79-horsepower motor, the Mack could cruise at 60 miles per hour and stop on a dime with its vacuum booster brakes. Occasionally driving it himself, Gus guided it down to Hot Springs.

His newly signed catcher almost didn't make it. Josh was on the bus bound for Hot Springs when he felt excruciating pain in his side. When it became unbearable, Josh was taken off the bus and rushed to a small hospital. His appendix had burst, and an operation was performed to remove it. It was a fairly routine matter even in 1932, but had he not been able to get to a hospital, had the attack come while the team was traveling in rural areas, it would have killed him.

As it was, his strength enabled him to recuperate quickly. After two weeks in bed, he was able to walk around. Finally he was released from the hospital and able to attend Crawford workouts. By mid-March he was still unable to play, and posed for a team picture in street clothes. His face was gaunt and he was noticeably thin, having lost close to twenty pounds during his stay in the hospital. But he was very alive, only twenty-one, and eager to swing a bat.

That spring was the first time many of the new Crawford players got to see Josh. Jimmie Crutchfield, Rap Dixon, Jud Wilson, and second-string catcher W. G. "Bill" Perkins had all played in other parts of the country and had only heard of "Samson" Gibson, the young slugger for the 1931 Homestead Grays. Josh started slowly and played himself into shape, gaining weight with each day. Yet it didn't take him long to show what he had. Manager Charleston put him in left field while Perkins caught, for Josh's bat, even in his weakened condition, was still overpowering.

The Craws were not members of any league and didn't wish to be. It was Greenlee's idea that there was more money to be made in Negro baseball if a team was able to expand its schedule throughout the season whenever it wished. (The theory had worked well with Posey and the Grays in the years before they joined the Negro National League.) Greenlee planned to travel all over, widening the scope of black ball, especially in the South. The Craws would play almost anybody and exhibit the best caliber of baseball possible. No longer would it be limited to Yankee Stadium, or the Pittsburgh area, or Chicago and Kansas City.

They began on March 25 in J. C. Stovall's Monroe, Louisiana. From there, with their well-equipped, comfortable bus, they toured the South, all the while sending back dispatches and news via the *Courier* to the fans back in Pittsburgh. John Clark traveled along as the team's secretary and informal historian. In comments interjected between box scores, he lamented the conditions of blacks still living in the South, how their districts were bordered by railroad sidings or cemeteries and were pockets of poverty. He marveled at the different conditions for blacks in Monroe, and in Houston, Texas, he complimented a Creole woman named Mother Mitchell who spoke no English but who earned a fortune—$25,000 a month— in oil. Mother Mitchell feted the entire ball club in her home and graciously entertained them. Satchel Paige and Sam Streeter responded to the treatment by pitching superbly against Houston teams.

As they traveled, the Craws' reputation grew. Gibson regained his strength with each game but stayed in left field. At the plate he hit everything that was thrown. Bill Perkins caught, receiving the best of Paige, who was then throwing almost nothing but scorching fastballs that reminded old-timers of the salad days of Smokey Joe Williams, Bullet Rogan, and Dick Redding.

Playing beside Josh in the outfield was Jimmie Crutchfield, a tiny but amazingly quick ballplayer whose size made him all the more determined to play well. Speed such as Crutchfield's was a common commodity among the Crawfords and one of the most noticeable aspects of Negro baseball. Even Gibson with his size was fast when he was young. In straight-out sprinting contests he could stay with anyone. On the base paths he was a constant base-stealing threat and ran with impunity. Yet he was most valuable for his power, the awesome drives that in 1932 added to a reputation that traveled far ahead of him. Behind him were the bats of Perkins, Charleston, Judy Johnson, Rap Dixon, and Jud Wilson. They gave the Crawfords a formidable lineup, a team that Gus Greenlee could flaunt.

As the spring weeks passed, the Crawford bus traveled all over the South. They players adapted well to each other, something which became less difficult with each game. From March 25 through July 21, the Craws played 94 games in 109 days. Thirteen games were rained out; only two days were open dates. The team bus, meanwhile, logged 17,000 miles. During that time, the team made its way north to Pittsburgh and prepared for the first of its many showdown series with the Grays. The Gray-Crawford games were to be enormous attractions heralded weeks ahead of time by excited *Courier* writers. The rivalry was not just geographical but also a test of the temperaments of Greenlee and Cum Posey. Both men dearly wanted to beat each other.

Posey, for all of his preseason blustering and obstinacy, assembled a superb Gray roster despite the loss to Greenlee of so many of his top players. He eagerly took the Grays into Greenlee Field in early May for a five-game Crawford series. Each game was a battle; the teams were evenly matched due to the youth and raw talent of the Crawfords, and Posey's tough, experienced, yet unsung Grays. The Crawfords managed to take three of five games, but they were hard-pressed to do it. Few Pittsburgh fans felt sorry for the losing Grays. Instead, they realized the beginning of a rivalry which would go on for years and supply some of the best baseball ever seen in that city.

The two teams went out of their way to attract big crowds,

even if it meant taking on Pennsylvania's blue laws. To tap the day's potential for profit, the teams once scheduled a Sunday game to begin at 12:01 A.M. Played under newly installed lights at Greenlee Field (at a cost to Gus of $6,000), the game was a nice success and attracted 3,000 "night people." It finally ended in a Gray win at 3:00 A.M.

Behind the scenes, the blooming of the Crawfords and Gus Greenlee was actually a much-needed boon to the Grays. Posey's club badly needed revenues from the series between the two teams. Times were so bad for league teams in 1932 that the entire East-West Negro league—Baltimore, Cleveland, Philadelphia's Hilldale, the Cuban Stars, Newark, and the Grays—broke up in late June. The last half of the season was canceled and players' salaries were cut off. The Grays had to scramble to pick up games where they could, a task made difficult because they had lost their grip on profitable outlying areas to the Crawfords.

Some saw the bad turn of events as a kind of justice to the dictatorial Posey. He was fighting for his baseball life, his league had collapsed, his players were raided "by the same ruthless methods he had used against other owners in past years," one Pittsburgh sportswriter declared. Like most other owners except Greenlee, Posey could not meet payroll checks and had to compensate his players with a percentage of the gate receipts. But worst of all, Posey was suffering professionally. Although his Grays beat the Crawfords ten of nineteen games in 1932, including one in which they came from a 9-3 deficit to win, 13-10, they fell from glory in the fans' eyes. Sportswriter Rollo Wilson wrote: "The Crawfords have taken the play away from the Grays and no longer do Smoky City fans consider Cum Posey's bunch the penultimate in baseball."

As gratifying as this was to Gus Greenlee—and few denied that his entrance into big-time baseball was to some degree spurred by the rivalry with Posey—his investment in the Crawfords was not returning him any considerable money. In fact, he wound up the season losing an estimated $16,000. Still, the Craws were making the best of bad times, and surviving in style where other Negro teams were starving.

For Josh and his teammates, the camaraderie of the road and the constant competition served to block out what financial hardship surrounded them. Traveling together in the Mack bus made the team a close-knit fraternity. When heat and exhaustion from the heavy schedule did not drive them into a dead-away sleep, the high times rolled through the bus. Because the Mack was roomy and comfortable, sleep came easily, especially after players consumed the bags of food—cold cuts, cheese, and pickles—they brought on board after the games.

Keeping one's food wasn't always easy. Jimmie Crutchfield remembers how each player put his sandwiches in the rack overhead and then drifted off to sleep. It was common practice for other players to swipe the sandwiches and pass them around. Everybody did it, yet the victim was burned up about it each time. One night, Harry Kincannon, a light-skinned pitcher (so much so that few felt he would have been challenged had he tried to crack a major-league lineup) who was called "Tincan," came aboard with a number of pieces of fried chicken. After he had eaten his fill, he stood up and showed the team a small pistol he had with him. The pistol actually belonged to Oscar Charleston, who had gotten it from a politician in Cuba. Kincannon flashed the gun and said, "Anybody eatin' my food tonight gonna get it from this." Then he put the pistol on his lap and fell asleep. While he slept, the pistol fell on the floor, and as one of the Crawfords emptied the shells from the gun, another passed Tincan's chicken around. They ate the chicken, then collected the bones and tied them into a necklace which they draped around the sleeping Kincannon. When he awoke and discovered his bony necklace, the team howled. Kincannon was outraged, but not enough to keep from laughing himself.

Such scenes were repeated over and over as the bus rolled up the miles. It was not uncommon to travel all night, from Chicago to Philadephia, or similar distances, to arrive in time to play a doubleheader. The bull sessions, the marathon pinochle games, the sleeping, the tricks and jokes were just a part of the routine, unforgettable to a bunch of black kids who would look back on those days as the best of their lives.

With what leisure time they did find, the team stayed mostly around the hotels or motor lodges playing cards or talking baseball. Josh was notorious for sitting in a hotel lobby and talking shop with Judy Johnson, Crutchfield, and the others. Small cliques of players formed. Josh usually fell in with Crutchfield, pitcher Leroy Matlock, and later Ted Page, Sammy Bankhead, Chester Williams, and Dick Seay. If they weren't playing cards, they went into town and had a beer. None of them had too much money to spend. When they did, they bought clothes or went dancing. Josh always had difficulty buying clothes that fit him well because he was so large in the chest and arms. It made him somewhat insecure about wearing new styles. Crutchfield and the others once had to coax him to buy a pair of plus fours, the rage at the time.

In small towns like Dormont, Pennsylvania, or Salamanca, New York, or countless others on the itinerary, the Crawfords were always an attraction, and often they found it difficult to have any privacy during off-hours. It was not uncommon for girls to huddle around the lobbies just to be near the players. The townsfolk often put on dances, sometimes outdoors under light, and the team and crowds of people turned out. As players such as Satchel Paige and Josh gained reputations, they attracted the girls. Satchel reveled in the attention, but Josh as a kid was shy, self-conscious, and not at all quick-witted or casual with his female fans. He was, however, a good dancer and his modesty and boyish good looks made him extremely likable and popular. His best times on the dance floor usually came at the expense of Harry Kincannon, who was a lousy dancer and got the brunt of Josh's razzing.

As popular and admired as touring teams such as the Crawfords were, the players' relationships with girls on the road seldom came to much. For the most part, the players were young, inexperienced boys raised in Baptist homes. The times made for strict, modest sexual attitudes. Later, many of the players married, and such arrangements occasionally became strained because of the travel and the attentions of other women. Yet the Crawfords, like almost all of the touring black teams, were anything but philanderers, and they would later look back on their out-of-town sexual ventures with modesty and restraint.

They were more concerned with the game they played, and the way they played it as Crawfords. Few owners put as much class into their organization as did Greenlee. He was free with money, though he didn't spoil anyone, and he treated his players so well that few were ever to speak badly of him. Uniforms and equipment were also first-rate and abundant, even to providing two bats for each player. Such seemingly minor frills as a surplus of bats were important to Negro teams, for many were so impoverished that players had to supply their own bats or borrow them from others. That the Crawfords came into town with clean, tailored uniforms, a team bus, a secretary, and a locker full of equipment amazed even fans in strong baseball towns. Such extravagance hadn't been seen since the early 1920s when Rube Foster's American Giant teams had traveled the country in their own Pullman cars and carried with them as many as five sets of uniforms. Greenlee's Crawfords weren't the major leagues, but the baseball they played and the class they exhibited rivaled the big time, and black fans everywhere knew it. The Craws were sensations. They won every series in 1932 but two—one in May to the Black Yankees, and another late in September to the Grays—and they compiled an unofficial record for the summer season of 99-36. There was no better team in Negro baseball. Yet the golden era of the Crawfords was just beginning.

5

Beisbol

There is a marvelous snapshot in Jimmie Crutchfield's scrapbook of a smiling, skinny Cool Papa Bell arriving in the Dominican Republic in 1937. Bell is carrying a stuffed satchel, wearing an open sport jacket and a wide-brimmed fedora tilted back on his head, and the bright, tropical sun casts his shadow against the bleached stone of the buildings. Thick-leaved potted plants are everywhere, most growing to a height above the slender, six-foot Cool Papa, who, aged thirty-two and one of Negro baseball's most poised performers, appears more than happy to be there.

There is a marvelous photo in Cool Papa Bell's scrapbook of him and a half dozen of his Pittsburgh Crawford teammates swimming in a river near Santo Domingo. They are not really swimming, but posing for a photo of a mock drowning of one of the players. The Crawfords are in skimpy swim trunks, their lean, muscular legs flailing everywhere, huddled around the supposedly stricken teammate who has flopped down on the dock with his tongue out and his eyes rolling upward. Yet the Craws are atrocious actors and cannot contain wide grins and the overwhelming urge to break up in laughter.

Still another photo in Cool Papa's book shows him and Josh outside their Santo Domingo locker room. In an awkward, posed picture, the two of them are looking down at a bat, and Josh is pointing toward the fat part of it as if to say that this is the end you don't hold. In script letters across the front of their uniforms is the name of the country's dictator, Trujillo.

Such are the memories of baseball played south of the border, in Mexico, Cuba, Venezuela, and Puerto Rico. Almost all American black ballplayers went from summer leagues to limited autumn and early winter competition in California or Texas, and finally traveled down south for the winter. The game they found there was hotter than the weather, producing not only exquisite baseball (*beisbol*) but rabid fans and national heroes.

A number of white major-and minor-league players from the States went south to work out problems, perfect skills—a new position, switch-hitting, a new delivery—or to play back into shape after an injury. It was the mark of a hardworking major leaguer that he spent his winter playing ball instead of fishing, and a must for a minor leaguer to go down there to improve himself. For black players, however, winter ball was a matter of necessity. They played because they needed the money. Their side of the profession knew no such thing as a vacation or an off-season. Starting in 1933, Josh went south each winter for most of his career. Almost all of his teammates joined him.

The most conspicuous aspect of winter baseball was the absence of a color line. Whites played with blacks, Puerto Ricans, Mexicans, and Cubans in front of Latin crowds. The only thing that came of it was good baseball and the obvious fact that America's color bar was based on myth, imagination, bad judgment, and timorous club owners. What unrest prevailed, racial or otherwise, usually concerned a good brawl with umpires, brief fistfights between players after a beanball, or a hard slide—something that all ballplayers, regardless of color, relished.

The winter leagues were also prime opportunities for whites to see just how good the black and Latin players were—if, of course, they didn't already know. After a few weeks of winter competition, after whites were struck out, thrown out, and outhit by their black and brown counterparts, none of them could honestly maintain that the best blacks and Latins weren't good enough to play in the big leagues, as owners and league officials up north were wont to suggest. A particularly good game often moved major-league players, and occasionally a club official, to venture to suggest to black stars like Paige, Bell, Gibson, and others how valuable they'd be if they were white. They threw out astounding figures. "I could afford to pay a hundred thousand dollars for you," Earl Mack of the Phillies told Bell in 1934. The same went for Josh, Satchel, Buck Leonard, and so many others, to the point where blacks tired of hearing such talk. "Yeah, sure," they'd reply, knowing through the years that such statements, in the face of Jim Crow, were not even compliments.

Latin fans (*franticos*), however, weren't as hypocritical. They were crazy about black American stars and packed the stands to cheer them. Foreign club owners, many of them politicians or wealthy businessmen, readily offered black players two and three times their American salaries to keep them coming south each winter. Mexican fans were the wildest, especially in the late 1930s and 1940s when baseball flourished there. They sometimes got so emotional that players worried about things getting out of control. Rival teams were pelted with produce. In heated games, with fans screaming in Spanish at anyone close to the action, players were even doused with the contents of bedpans.

Yet black players gladly tolerated the antics of Latin fans. Packed stadiums made for fat salaries. Off the field, players were idolized and shown none of the discrimination they saw as a matter of course in the States. They were treated as celebrities on many occasions, were free to go anywhere, eat anywhere, and do anything. They had no feelings of apprehension or the instinctive hesitation that a black had before he did anything or went anywhere in white America. Players did not live that well, for in the early days of Cuban, Puerto Rican, and Mexican baseball the luxury accommodations those countries would later build for tourists did not exist. Players considered their lodgings second class by most standards, yet they seldom if ever complained. They were conditions better than those they had to endure in the States: fleabag hotels so rancid that players sometime slept in chairs rather than risk lying with what was crawling in the beds.

When the hard times of the Depression further weakened American Negro ball, foreign leagues became increasingly attractive. A number of top stars not only played full winter seasons down south but accepted offers to stay there through the summer season. The money was the main attraction, yet the social benefits were not to be denied.

"I came back to play ball for Vera Cruz [in the Mexican League] because I have a better future in Mexico than in the States," said Willie Wells, a superb shortstop for the Newark Eagles to *Courier* sportswriter Wendell Smith. Wells went on to say that he didn't deserve the adverse publicity he was getting because of his decision. In a lengthy, candid interview, Wells summed up the feelings of many American black stars who felt at home in foreign countries:

Not only do I get more money playing here, but I live like a king . . . in the first place, I am not faced with the racial problem of Mexico. When I travel with Vera Cruz we live in the best hotels, we eat in the best restaurants and can go anyplace we care to. You know as well as other Negroes that we don't enjoy such privileges in the United States. We stay in any kind of hotel, far from the best, and eat only where we know we will be accepted. Until recently Negro players in the United States had to go all over the country in buses, while in Mexico we've always traveled in trains . . . We have everything first class here, plus the fact that the people here are much more considerate than the American baseball fan. I mean that we are heroes here, and not just ballplayers. . . . I was going to stay in the States and play for Newark, but I think a ballplayer, or any working man, should take advantage of better opportunities. I didn't quit Newark and join some other team in the States. I quit and left the country. . . . I've found freedom and democracy here, something I never found in the United States. I was branded a Negro in the States and had to act accordingly. Everything I did, including playing ball, was regulated by my color.

Well, here in Mexico I am a man. I can go as far in baseball as I am capable of going. I can live where I please and will encounter no restrictions of any kind because of my race. So, you see, that also had a lot to do with my decision to return here.

Wells added that in Mexico he was known as "El Diablo," "the Devil." "It's a pet name," he told Smith. "That's what they're calling me back in Newark, too. But they don't mean it the same way."

Those players who didn't feel as strongly about foreign ball as did Wells nonetheless had to admit that they enjoyed the winter life-style. They found themselves with a luxurious amount of leisure time. The leagues did not involve a lot of traveling, at least not the amount black players were accustomed to. Long, lazy hours were spent playing pinochle and eating ice cream in hotel rooms and lobbies. Players went swimming and clowned for pictures; they fished, rented boats, or just spent time in the sun.

In Cuba, where winter ball first flourished in the early 1920s, and then again in the late 1930s, teams such as Mariana, Almendares, Havana, and Cienfuegos were allowed only four American players on each club. These were usually the best of the Negro leagues, and their exploits were reported in the large black newspapers back in the States. The Cubans had their own stars, such as Luis Tiant (whose son, Luis, Jr., later became a fine major-league pitcher), along with Cuban players who performed in American Negro leagues during the summer season. The Cubans even had a touring House of David team, patterned after the popular, bearded Original House of David team from southwestern Michigan. Apart from their thick beards, the Cuban version bore no resemblance to the real thing, except for the quality of baseball they played.

Cuban ball was as raucous as any south of the border. American black players go into more fights with the Cubans than anybody else. The brawls were wild and nasty, often inciting the fans to break from the crowd and start swinging. In most Cuban parks, police officers stood at the corners of the grandstands to keep the spectators from going onto the field. Chicken wire was even placed above the fences. In one 1934 game, the Cuban cops could not handle the players. Josh became so embroiled in a fight that two officers jumped him and tried to pull him out of a pile of kicking, slugging players. Each officer grabbed an arm, but Josh lifted them both into the air and threw them off. They then dove onto his legs and held on while Josh walked from home plate all the way to second base in pursuit of a Cuban whose head he dearly wanted to crack.

Off the field, the American black players once again found themselves able to mingle freely with the natives even though they knew little of the language. "When you get hungry enough," Josh once told his sister, "you find yourself speaking Spanish pretty well."

He told another story of a time he mistakenly left $50 in a suit he sent out to be pressed. When he suddenly missed the money, he ran down to the tailor shop to get it. When he got there, he discovered that the tailor had lost his ability to understand English. The two of them argued excitedly until Josh realized he was getting nowhere. He then reached over the counter with one hand, grabbed the tailor by the throat, and lifted him into the air.

"All of a sudden," Josh said later, "that tailor spoke better English than I did. I got my fifty bucks."

He told the story over and over again in the years following, and each time it broke him up so that he bellowed with his deep laughter.

In the 1930s, black players were traveling mostly to Puerto Rico for winter ball. They were some of the first Americans to play there instead of in Cuba, where political strife in that decade severely affected the leagues and the fans' ability to safely attend games. The trip to Puerto Rico wasn't an easy one. From

New York, it took five days by boat to get to San Juan. Once there, the players branched out on teams representing Santurce, Ponce, Mayaguez, Humacao, Aguadilla, Caguas, and Guayama, with San Juan the center of attraction. There teams played in Escambron Park, built in the heart of the city in 1932, with a seating capacity of 32,000. It was not unusual for every seat to be filled for the Saturday and Sunday games featuring all-star teams or league contests with the best of the white, Latin, and black stars who had invaded the island for the season.

Though Puerto Rico, with its tropical breezes and sparkling coral reefs, remained a prime spot for winter ball through the years, the Mexican leagues became popular with players in the late 1930s and and 1940s. The Mexican teams were richer than Puerto Rican or Cuban clubs, and often came up with salary offers three and four times those of the American Negro leagues.

It was an appetizing package, for as Willie Wells pointed out, ballplayers lived and traveled in the style of white major leaguers and they encountered no segregated trains, water fountains, restaurants, or hotels. Even so, conditions weren't always the best. Outside Mexico City, the water was unreliable, and players who were not careful became sick overnight. The heat at times became unbearable, and with no air conditioning, players found little relief. They exhausted themselves on the playing field after just a few innings of play. Some of the bus rides between towns involved treacherous trips through mountains where winding two-lane roads barely held the swaying team bus, and players inside went pale with fright.

Mexico hosted several postseason games between touring American teams, sometimes entire squads, such as the Crawfords, or loosely organized Negro league All-Star teams, and major-league All-Star teams. It made no difference to Mexican fans, for they were elated with the visitors' play. They packed the stadium in Mexico City one day in late October 1935 for a game between the Crawfords and a major-league squad made

Rare postcard photo taken in early 1900s of Andrew "Rube" Foster, the Father of Negro Baseball. Standing second from left, Foster was pitcher, then manager of a team he organized, the Chicago American Giants. Also pictured are league officials F. Knox Howard, J. D. Howard, and manager of the Indianapolis ABC's, Charles I. Taylor.

Young Josh (seated, second from left), surrounded by some of the best of the 1932 Crawfords. Standing, player-manager Oscar Charleston was a strict, demanding coach and a versatile, valuable first baseman considered one of the best ever in the Negro leagues. From left, Rap Dixon, Josh, Judy Johnson, and Jud Wilson. They were the meat of the Crawford lineup that year even though Dixon and Wilson stayed with the team only a short time. Johnson, a Hall-of-Famer, as are Josh and Charleston, was with the Crawfords throughout the team's finest years.

(Photo courtesy of James "Cool Papa" Bell)

Gus Greenlee's first Crawford contender, spring training, 1932, in Hot Springs, Arkansas. The year marked the beginning of the Crawfords as one of the best, most stylish black teams in the country. Josh posed out of uniform, having been recently released from a hospital where he underwent an appendectomy. He was somewhat gaunt and underweight and about to play himself back into shape.

Kneeling (left to right): Sam Streeter, Chester Williams, Harry Williams, Harry Kincannon, Henry Spearman, Jimmie Crutchfield, Bobby Williams, Ted "Double Duty" Radcliffe.
Standing (left to right): Owner Gus Greenlee, T. Jones, L. D. Livingston, Satchel Paige, Gibson, Roy Williams, Walter "Rev" Cannady, Bill Perkins, Oscar Charleston, club secretary John Clark.

(Photo courtesy of Jimmie Crutchfield)

Decked out and ready to ramble, Josh, Leroy Matlock, and Jimmie Crutchfield sport caps and "plus fours," the rage of 1934. Photo was taken in Philadelphia.

(Photo courtesy of Jimmie Crutchfield)

The 1935 Crawfords, again during spring training in Hot Springs, Arkansas.
Standing (left to right): Jelly Taylor, Judy Johnson, Leroy Matlock, unknown rookie, Josh Gibson, Hood Witton, trainer.
Seated: Cool Papa Bell, Sam Bankhead, Oscar Charleston, Clarence Palm, Jimmie Crutchfield, Spoon Carter, Bill Perkins.
Seated on ground: T. Bond, Howard, Nat Hunter, Sam Streeter, Harry Kincannon, Duro Davis.

(Photo courtesy of Jimmy Crutchfield)

The power that was Josh. Taken during Gibson's prime years
with the Homestead Grays, this photo captures the power
and grace of Josh's batting style. Former Negro league
players who played with and against Josh remember him best
this way.

(Photo courtesy of Bill Yancey)

The 1936 Pittsburgh Crawfords pose at the beginning of the season in front of the team's Mack touring bus. In the background is Greenlee Field in Pittsburgh, the finest Negro baseball park in the country. This team, with five major league Hall of Famers in the lineup—Oscar Charleston, Josh Gibson, Satchel Paige, Judy Johnson, Cool Papa Bell—was considered by many to be one of the finest squads ever assembled, regardless of color.

Kneeling (left to right): Oscar Charleston, Jimmie Crutchfield, Dick Seay, Sam Bankhead, Bill Harvey, Sam Streeter, Bill Perkins, Chester Williams, Theolic "Fireball" Smith, Harry Kincannon, Judy Johnson, Cool Papa Bell, Leroy Matlock, Ernest "Spoon" Carter, Josh Gibson, John Washington, Satchel Paige, unknown rookie pitcher.

(Photo courtesy of Jimmie Crutchfield)

With Josh Gibson

Josh and Cool Papa Bell in the Dominican Republic, 1937.
Uniforms reveal team name and owner of the club, Rafael
Trujillo, who also happened to be president of the Dominican Republic. His political fortunes were closely tied to the
popularity and success of his baseball team, hence the
presence of American stars like Gibson, Bell, Satchel Paige,
and others greatly improved his popular standing.

(Photo courtesy of James "Cool Papa" Bell)

The Old Pros. A collection of former Negro league players posed for pictures during a reunion in Chicago in 1972.

Standing (left to right): Carter Wilson, Perry Hall, Ted Radcliffe, Alex Radcliffe, Subby Byas, Cool Papa Bell, Jack Marshall.

Middle row: Hannibal Cox, Sugar Cornelius, David Malarcher, Ted Page, Jelly Gardner, Jew Baby Bennett.

Front: Maurice Wiggins, Jimmie Crutchfield, Bobby Anderson, Clarence Jones.

(Photo courtesy of Jimmie Crutchfield)

up of such players as Jimmie Foxx, Rogers Hornsby, Heinie Manush, Pinky Higgins, and Earl Whitehill.

With the Crawfords' Leroy Matlock facing Whitehill, the game was closely played. The major leaguers pushed ahead, 4-2, after eight innings of play. In the top of the ninth, Sammy Bankhead led off with a triple. Clarence "Spoony" Palm, a catcher playing with the Craws in the off-season, batted for Matlock and tied the score with a clutch home run to left field. The hit unnerved Whitehill, and he gave up two more runs for a Crawford lead of 6-4 going into the last half of the ninth.

The story at this point serves to illustrate an almost unavoidable problem in researching the history of Negro baseball. The results of this game were first related to me by a former Crawford, who said that in the last half of the ninth, Craw pitcher Roosevelt Davis got two men out, then caused Heinie Manush to ground back to him. In what would have been the game-ending play, Davis tossed the ball to Oscar Charleston at first. The normally flawless Charleston caught the ball on the heel of his glove, bobbled it as it rolled up his arm, and by the time he'd got hold of it, Manush was safely across the bag. That brought up the powerful Jimmie Foxx, who promptly lost one of Davis's pitches beyond the fence and tied the score. After the next hitter was retired, according to the former Crawford, the umpire quickly jumped out in front of home plate and said the game was called because of darkness.

Actually, a much different play occurred. According to a colorful story in the Mexican newspaper *La Afición,* the game went into two extra innings and was actually halted after a wild argument that ended in favor of the Crawfords.

Eleventh inning. The Crawfords could not score. The Stars came now for their half of the inning.

Kennedy who was now pitching for the Stars opened by flying out to left field. It was kind of dark. Everybody knew it was impossible to have another inning played and the Stars put in that inning all they had.

McNair got on base. Cramer too. Manush also and Foxx went to bat again.

We were all hoarse of so much yelling: "Hold that line." . . .

The grandstand fans, where the Stars are big favorites, were yelling, "Come on, Jimmie." . . .

But everybody was on his feet. The umpires' calls were lost in the noise. Nobody could hear them. Finally Foxx got hold of the ball and sent a terrific smash over third base. Johnson got hold of it, dropped it, picked it up. McNair was running near the third bag back and forth.

Finally he ran home. And here came the trouble. Johnson with the ball already in his possession went over his bag. Some fans say he touched it with his foot, and the force at home plate was taken away.

Johnson threw to Gibson. The latter stepped on the plate without touching McNair who came rushing from third.

The umpire called him out and the fireworks began. The Stars claimed McNair was safe, had legally scored, and Cramer was out at third when Johnson had stepped on his bag forcing him out.

The colored boys claimed Cramer was not out as Johnson had not stepped on his bag. The force out had been on McNair at home.

On the field and on the bleachers everybody took sides. . . . I have never seen so many baseball rule books.

But the umpire's ruling stood. Hornsby ended the inning by grounding out, and the game was then called because of darkness. Clusters of fans and players remained on the field arguing about the call. But the score held at 6-6, and it had been the Crawfords, not the white All-Stars, who had been saved by the umpires.

Like the other Latin countries, Mexico presented problems for players unable to stay out of trouble, keep away from women, and lay off the bottle. In February 1931, Willie Bobo, a first baseman for the Nashville Elite Giants, went to Tijuana after playing a winter-league game in San Diego, California. Bobo, who was called "the black George Sisler" after the famous St. Louis Browns first baseman, had been hit on the side of the head with a beanball during the game and decided to recuperate over a drink in Mexico, where booze was legal. Bobo's tastes in liquor, however, weren't the best, and he was found dead in his Tijuana hotel room. Next to his body was a bottle of what his teammates described charitably as "cheap alcohol."

For Josh, it was Puerto Rico that he grew most fond of. From his first season down there in 1933, he was an overwhelming hero to local fans. They were amazed at his quiet, awesome power, and they packed the stands to watch him. He obliged them by hitting grand home runs. San Juan's Escambron Stadium had an outfield wall ringed by trees growing about 50 feet back. Josh often nailed drives that disappeared into the trees, distances close to 500 feet away in the heavy tropical air. After each one, a stadium worker was sent climbing the high branches to hang a glittering marker on the spot where each fly ball was last seen. The markers stayed there for years, dotting the trees like Christmas tree ornaments. A more permanent monument was later put in center field. It was a stone tablet much like those erected in Yankee Stadium's center field for Babe Ruth and Lou Gehrig. Josh's marker was simple and inexpensive, but to the Puerto Ricans it was as sincere a tribute to the quiet giant from Pittsburgh as was New York's bronze monument to their Babe.

Josh was charmed by the reception he got in Puerto Rico and for the rest of his life would look upon his achievements there as the high point in his career. In the winter of 1941 he was honored as the league's most valuable player and batting champion. In ceremonies filled with speeches and wild applause, the league gave him a three-foot-high trophy. No most-valuable-player awards were given in the Negro leagues, and the honor was important to Josh.

But quiet pleasures in Puerto Rico also meant something to him. Josh spent long hours talking baseball with "Perucho" Cepeda, the island's native baseball hero, who was known as "the Bull" to fans. They compared stories in the presence of Cepeda's son, Orlando, a boy who would grow into his own as a ballplayer and star as "the Baby Bull" in American major-league competition.

As rewarding as winter baseball was, as attractive as the conditions and salaries were south of the border, few players, black or white, stayed down there much past March. Willie Wells, for all of his strong sentiments, played in Mexico only three years. The action was still up north, in the Midwest and East, where Negro baseball was played hard in front of home fans. Players looked forward to getting back together with their families even if their home lives were often fragmented and superficial. Josh, Paige, Bell, Leonard, and most of the others never felt comfortable wearing uniforms with names on the front which they could barely pronounce. They were Grays, Crawfords, Black Yankees—and their mettle was tested best back home.

6

One Dollar for a Thousand Songs

"Wake up and live! Stand up and shout! Yowsah! And howsah; it's a wowsah! Christmas day with the four stars, Horace Henderson, Orlando Robeson, Arthur Lee Simkins, and that little man with the big band, Don Redman. . . . All the Bronzeville guys and gals, stream-lined, thin, and fat, fell in for a cut of the 'Big Apple.'

"Among those present were Joseph 'Esquire' Hardy with the latest tails on from old man Kuppenheimer, high hat, cape, and all the trimmings. . . .

"Listen to that boy croon! Who's that? Oh! That's Joe 'Nagisaki' Williams who croons just like Bing Crosby. But the only difference between Bing and Joe is, Bing gets one thousand dollars for one song, Joe gets one dollar for a thousand songs. So you see, none but the brave deserve the 'Foo' and a happy Foo Year to you, Joe."

So rang the voice of Willard Cole from Chicago's Savoy Ballroom after a Depression Christmas and a New Year's Day wingding in that city's Black and Tan District. They were high times but cheap ones, usually lasting only until the sun came up and the hard times walked in for breakfast. Even Gus Greenlee in Pittsburgh, whose problems during the Depression were hardly those of most blacks, faced the new year of 1933 with austerity.

Although he had found much popular success by keeping the Crawfords officially out of the Negro leagues in 1932 and barnstorming with them around the country, Greenlee decided the following year to take a part in reorganizing the Negro leagues. He fully intended to build a new league as strong as the

81

one Rube Foster had operated in the 1920s. He also planned to head it himself, believing that his business prowess and his strong operating hand were enough to make it a success. In January he met with other team owners and formed the new Negro National League. It included the Crawfords, Cum Posey's Grays, the Detroit Stars, the reorganized Indianapolis ABCs, the Columbus Bluebirds, and the Chicago American Giants, then owned by Robert Cole.

Greenlee and the other owners were not overly optimistic. The new year, Greenlee said, "was a crucial time for the game. One thing is certain—there will be no big salaries for any of the players this season." If the general economic picture wasn't the owners' guide on the salary issue, the major leagues were. That year, Judge Kenesaw Mountain Landis, the commissioner of baseball, announced he was taking a salary cut. Babe Ruth also took one, from $75,000 to $50,000, despite highly publicized yowling from the Babe.

The cut came only months after Ruth's celebrated "pointed" home run in the 1932 World Series against the Chicago Cubs. Controversy arose over whether or not Babe had pointed to the bleachers in the fifth inning, thereby announcing the home run that was to follow, or if he merely put up one finger as if to say, "It takes only one," and then managed to park Charlie Root's next pitch in the stands. Hosts of baseball writers and biographers have researched the event, but none have discovered yet another version. According to black reporters at the game in Wrigley Field that October, one Amos "Loudmouth" Latimer was in the stands that day, as he was for almost every baseball game played in Comiskey Park or Wrigley Field. Latimer was considered the premier heckler of Chicago and a master mouth among the street-corner politicians along Forty-seventh Street in the South Side black district. Visiting outfielders dreaded Latimer and his tongue, and that included the Babe. After Babe hit a first-inning homer in the 1932 Series game, he returned to right field and Latimer's abuse. Loudmouth called him a bum, among other things, and threw lemon peels at him. Ruth finally turned around and gestured at Latimer, pointing his finger at him as if to say the next home run was coming his way. In the fifth inning against Root, Babe approached the plate, took off his cap, and waved it at Latimer. A few pitches later, he pointed that famous finger, the same way he'd done it earlier at Loudmouth, and, in the minds of many, in Latimer's direction. The home run he hit on Root's next pitch traveled 440 feet to center field, a tremendous line drive that landed 3 feet away from Loudmouth. Everyone in the bleachers—and most definitely Loudmouth Latimer—was certain of it, and howled about how Loudmouth had done it again. The story was passed along Forty-seventh Street for years afterward.

The new austerity in baseball, however, now affecting white as well as black leagues, was enough in the minds of Greenlee and fellow Negro-league owners to keep black players intimidated as far as money was concerned. Yet the owners were nagged by another problem, the poor attendance on the part of black fans at Negro-league games. It wasn't uncommon, owners lamented, for black teams to play in front of crowds made up mostly of whites. In cities where the white major-league teams played poorly, such as in Cincinnati in the 1930s, white fans often went to black games just to see good baseball, "to watch them monkeys play," as they often put it. White patronage was fine, but goodly numbers of blacks brought in the profits, and black owners planned to drop 1933 ticket prices in an effort to encourage more black fans to show up.

If Greenlee was to be successful in his new league venture, he believed, he had to instill a sense of organization in the Negro circuits. Because of haphazard organization in previous years, players had little respect for contracts, league rules, or league personnel. Umpires usually bore the brunt of it, for without a strong league structure behind them, they could hardly keep order. Players freely cursed and argued with umpires, sometimes to the point of pushing and punching them. When Vic Harris, the feisty Homestead Gray outfielder, attacked umpire Jimmie Ahern during an argument, Ahern was hard-pressed to retaliate in any other way than by filing criminal charges of assault and battery against Harris. The case was finally dropped, but it clearly demonstrated the seriousness of the situation and the weakness of the league as a disciplinary force.

When fans joined in what was then called "ragging" the ump, no amount of abuse was spared. Umpires literally feared for their safety and vowed to take measures to protect themselves. Some promised to pack pistols. Willie Wells, the Newark shortstop, once argued heatedly with an umpire in St. Louis, only to suddenly drop his bat and sprint for the third-base bleachers, where he jumped the fence and disappeared. The umpire had reached into his back pocket while jawing with Wells, and when Willie saw him do it, he was certain the umpire was going for a gun. Once Willie was out of sight, the umpire pulled out a whisk broom instead of a pistol, and went about brushing off home plate.

An umpire in Lylerly, Georgia, however, actually drew a pistol when the abuse became too much for him. He pointed it in the direction of the crowd and fired. Though nobody was hit, the fans were quiet suddenly. The umpire, meanwhile, was taken off to jail.

The umpiring problem was one all the owners, even Posey and Greenlee, could agree on. Posey wrote about players he considered "umpire baiters," and insisted they be dealt with. Jelly Gardner, the Chicago American Giants outfielder, was one of the worst, as far as Posey was concerned. "He kicked on every pitch," Cum wrote. "I frequently speak of Jelly with his ability to bunt, wait, and squabble as the only man I ever saw in baseball who could steal first base."

Player conduct and umpiring problems were symptomatic of the overall weaknesses in black baseball which Greenlee's new league had somehow to overcome. It was one thing to be able to pay ballplayers; it was another to discipline them and make league rules stick. At the beginning of the 1933 season, the new NNL was hard-pressed to do either.

The new season, however, promised nothing but the best as far as the individual Crawfords were concerned. With almost two years' worth of Greenlee's financial and personnel input, the club was strong and getting stronger, experienced, and convinced that the superlatives fans and sportswriters were doling out to them were deserved. They were the Yankees of black baseball, the slickest, most powerful, most polished team in the game, and their arrival in town was an *attraction*, not just another exhibition, not just another pickup between "them monkeys."

Josh, though only twenty-two, was now a prominent figure in sportswriters' vocabularies. It had taken some doing, a number of unforgettable clouts in the 1931 and 1932 seasons, to challenge the stature of some of the game's established sluggers. It helped that Louis "Top" Santop, the powerful catcher for the Lincoln Giants and Philadelphia's Hilldale club, had retired, for Santop had been called "the black Babe Ruth" for years because of 500-foot drives he'd stroked in stadiums all over the country.

Another reputation not so easy to overcome was that of George "Mule" Suttles, the glowering, stocky first baseman for Chicago's American Giants. Suttles was ten years older than Josh, built just like him, and possessed of much of the same power. Throughout the 1920s, he, too, was called "the black Babe Ruth" by his hometown writers. In fact, they claimed, Mule hit sixty-nine home runs in 1929 when he played for the St. Louis Stars, nine more than Ruth's mark, and that left little doubt in many minds that Mule was the greatest power hitter alive. Suttles was not a high-average hitter but one of the most dangerous clutch hitters in the game, and at the beginning of 1933 his fearsome power and incredible smashes against the upper decks of Comiskey Park, Yankee Stadium, and other big-league parks made him, not Josh, the number-one black slugger.

Yet Josh was a comer and everyone knew it. His affability and desire made him better with each game. He was easy to manage—about all you had to do, his teammates often said, was to put his name in the starting lineup and forget about things— and easy to instruct. Although he was still quiet and generally modest, he began to develop a sense of style that complemented his power and appealed to the fans. To the delight of everyone, he often stepped out of the box during a tight duel with a pitcher and turned up the bill of his cap. With that, and with his sleeves rolled up above his biceps, his long, heavy, menacing bat wiggling above his head, he was a joy to watch. Pitchers to a man respected him. Chet Brewer, the tough (and tough for Josh) pitcher for the Monarchs and the American Giants, said that Josh was the "type of fellow you immediately got the urge to 'trap,' " to set up and fool. But it was difficult because Josh had such control and balance as a hitter.

Besides Josh, the Craws still had the uncompromising Oscar Charleston as player-manager. Judy Johnson was at third base, and Ted Page and Crutchfield, along the the newly signed Cool Papa Bell, were in the outfield. On the mound were such tough pitchers as lefty Sam Streeter, Harry Kincannon, William Bell, Leroy Matlock, and the one and only Satchel Paige.

Paige, by this time, had established himself as one of the characters of the game: an unpredictable, witty, ornery, wise-cracking, but superbly talented pitcher. He was an attraction and he knew it, so much so that in coming years he would defy Greenlee over and over again by jumping from the club and playing for someone else. He once jumped to a team in South Dakota, played there and earned a big salary, then jumped back to the Crawfords. Greenlee was enraged, as he invariably would be, but he accepted Satchel and put him back on the mound, even protected him from sheriff's deputies from South Dakota who had come to Pittsburgh intent on returning Paige to their hometown club.

Paige's lapses also lost him favor with sportswriters. After a 1932 game against Brooklyn's Bushwick club in which Satchel was roundly knocked out of the box, writers insisted that his poor performance was due to his carousing. Paige, a writer said, had been "living it up" the night before the game and hadn't had the stamina to perform. As good as Satchel was, it was claimed, he had permitted himself to fall out of shape and was unprepared to take on the tough black clubs. "It is an old and true story of the Negro athlete," the writer went on. "When he is good he figures he is invaluable to his owner. He pulls all sorts of things, apparently secure in the belief that he cannot be replaced. Negro baseball has always been at the mercy of carousing stars."

Yet Satchel never fell out of grace with anyone for long. He was the best copy black sportswriters had. They hovered about him and were amply rewarded with entertaining nonsense. "I was born with control. I take two awful hot baths a day. I keep moving all the time on the diamond and I eat nothing but fried foods," he'd babble. Then he went out and did it, no matter how difficult the opposition, and returned for the publicity, the girls, the money, the clothes, the cars.

Almost from the beginning of their careers, Paige and Gibson were grouped together. They were exquisite examples of totally different talents—Satchel, the gangling, whip-armed pitcher; Josh, the stocky, mean-eyed power hitter. They possessed opposite personalities, especially as Satchel, "the sports world's darling," developed his ability to jive and entertain on the field and off, and Josh, "the player's player," crashed longer, more awesome drives, yet ran them out in silence. In more ways than as pitcher and catcher, Satchel threw, Josh received.

Although Josh and Satchel were able to thrive off each other—each making the Crawfords of the 1930s a formidable club—Paige was in many ways a serious blow to Josh's professional fortunes. Neither of them ever said much about it, but there was really no way that Josh could come out ahead as long as he played with Satchel Paige. Satchel was the crowd-getter, the moneymaker, the feature writer's dream. He was also a star, a pitcher capable of bearing down and vanquishing anyone, throwing what Josh called "Satchel's peaball," because it was no bigger than that. He was a pitcher's pitcher as much as Josh was a hitter's hitter. And though Josh gained respect from baseball men for his ability to hit for an average, to help a club with his speed and his glove, to hit the ball *hard*, he could not come close to being the attraction that Paige was by the simple fact of Paige's scintillating presence.

Few players ever talked about it or complained of it, but they did have certain misgivings about the attention Paige received. The publicity, coupled with the nature of Paige's personality, kept him from being a close friend to the other Crawfords. In fact, he was very much a loner, a player his teammates saw on the field but seldom off. Josh, on the other hand, was always close to his teammates, at dances, card games, or just hanging around. As great as he was, Josh endeared himself to his teammates because he never shoved his greatness in their faces. Satchel, even if subconsciously, did it all the time.

Still, Satchel's teammates were not the type to speak out against him, not then or years later. They liked to call him "just a big, overgrown little boy," or by one of his apt nicknames, "Dogface," and left it at that. Josh, in his usual manner, said nothing at all. Greenlee enjoyed them both. He feted Josh behind the plate and publicized his bat; he primed Satchel for tough games and big events, even loaned him out for exhibitions. Yet Greenlee could not deny the competition between the two through the years. Finally, in the eyes of Cum Posey, it "became so evident that Josh had to be traded."

When they played against each other, either during winter leagues or in later years, Josh and Satchel kept their rivalry in strict baseball terms. Satchel said Josh was the best hitter in baseball but that he knew Josh's weakness: "If he can't see the ball, he can't hit it." Josh replied that he could hit for a .400 average against Satchel in regular play, and .700 "in the pinches." On the field, the two occasionally needled each other. Once when Josh belted a Paige pitch out of the park, he yelled out to the mound as he rounded the bases, "If you could cook, I'd marry ya." But mostly the two men played around each other. Satchel went on his own as he had always done. Josh, knowing he was no match for Satchel's wit and style, continued to communicate mostly with his awesome bat.

The Crawfords proceeded to overwhelm league opponents and travel about in search of lucrative engagements. They once played a team which featured the legendary female athlete Babe Didrikson. She pitched and proved a tough test for the Craws, who at first took her lightly and then found themselves fanning on her excellent breaking pitches. The team also took every opportunity to play against the House of David team, the religious, black-bearded club from Michigan. Just as it was often speculated that numbers of blacks would be signed by major-league clubs if the color ban were lifted, so the House of David players, called "Whiskers" by Negro teams, were considered pro material if they should ever consent to shave their beards, as major-league teams would no doubt require. A few did, such as Bullet Ben Benson, who signed with the Washington Senators in 1934. He lasted only two games, lost one, and gave up a total of nineteen hits in ten innings.

Back in Pittsburgh, Greenlee kept a tough eye on his rackets. His numbers still provided the cash, the Crawford Grille remained a magnet which drew athletes, entertainers, gamblers, and politicians. Gus threw Christmas parties at the Grille which were enormous affairs and attracted people from all over Pennsylvania. With his popularity came power, and Gus rose to take political control of Pittsburgh's black Third Ward, which he held for years. Light-heavyweight champion John Henry Lewis was one of Greenlee's many boxers, and when the Crawfords weren't playing in Greenlee Field, Gus scheduled fight cards there.

But none of his enterprises brought as much attention as did his drive to stage a Negro baseball All-Star game. The idea came from Roy Sparrow, one of Gus's employes who thought of it in 1932, a year before the first major-league All-Star game was played. In 1933, with his hand on 10 percent of the gate, Gus set up the first East-West Negro League All-Star game at Chicago's Comiskey Park. Little did he or anyone else know that it was to be the start of the most celebrated, best-attended, and most glamorous event in the history of Negro baseball.

The All-Star game fascinated the fans in part because of the very weaknesses of the Negro leagues. It superseded attempts at league World Series games because after seasons rife with weak franchises, shaky scheduling, and uneven competition, series games were seldom a test of the best team in Negro baseball so much as finals for teams with the richest or most influential owners. But the All-Star game was a stage on which an individual player could shine, no matter how weak or how bad the team he played for. It also was a chance for fans to vote for their personal stars. Voting was conducted through big-city black newspapers and hence was often dominated by players from teams in towns like Pittsburgh, Chicago, and New York. In fact, the All-Star rosters in 1933 consisted mostly of Chicago American Giants on the West team, and Crawfords and Grays on the East.

The game attracted only 8,000 fans (that figure varied through the years from 8,000 to 40,000) to Comiskey Park, but it was a colorful, hotly played game that promised to get bigger and better. The West won it 11-7, battering the Crawfords' Sam Streeter for seven runs in six innings. Josh got only a base hit, and was outshone by Mule Suttles, who hit the game's only home run deep into the seats. Gibson also showed poorly when he attempted to pick Sammy Bankhead of the Nashville Elite

Giants off first base. His throw was late and wild and skipped into foul territory behind the bullpen in right field. Bankhead went into second and sprinted for third, then decided to challenge the throw from the East's right fielder and slid into home for an unearned run.

The popularity of the first game, however, convinced Greenlee and other league officials that the East-West rivalry was there to stay. Apart from the keen moments surrounding local rivalries such as the Gray-Crawford series in Pittsburgh, no single game was a better attraction or better served to kindle the imaginations of black baseball fans all over the country. They anticipated it weeks ahead of time, then swarmed on Comiskey Park. And their sportswriters rose to the occasion.

Before the 1934 game, the *Courier*'s Chester Washington wrote:

> Despite the fact that "East is East and West is West," the twain SHALL meet—on historic Comiskey Field—this Sunday!
> Carrying on their rosters two of the most brilliant aggregations of ballplayers ever assembled, the stellar East team and the formidable West club, representing the cream of the nation's current diamond crop as picked by the fans, promise to furnish one of the most thrilling baseball dramas ever enacted.

Washington then proceeded to list the players, preceding each with an adjective or three: "the brilliant Slim Jones . . . the strong-armed Bill Holland . . . the hard-hitting Josh Gibson . . . the colt-like Cool Papa Bell." And Washington saved a paragraph for Satchel Paige, again a mark of how popular Paige already was by 1934 and how his presence readily eclipsed Gibson's.

> If 30,000 attend, 29,999 will be hoping to see the slow-moving fastball-pitching Satchell [*sic*] Paige, hero of the recent Denver *Post* Tourney, in action. "Satch," who won three games in five days out in Mile High City, in addition to being a great speedball pitcher is one of the best natural showmen in baseball. He is to Negro baseball today what Babe Ruth and Carl Hubbell were to the majors in yesteryears.

In front of 25,000 fans, Satchel lived up to his billing. In an evenly played game, the score remained 0-0 for six innings, when the West's Willie Wells doubled with nobody out. Washington described the rest of the inning like this:

> Pandemonium reigned in the West's cheering sections. An instant later a hush fell upon the crowd as the mighty Satchel Paige, prize "money" pitcher for the East, leisurely ambled across the field toward the pitcher's box. It was a dramatic moment. Displaying his picturesque double wind-up and nonchalant manner, Satchel started shooting 'em across the plate, and in five tosses fanned Radcliffe. The East's supporters breathed a sigh of relief and Satchel settled down to his task. "Turkey" Stearns flied out to Vic Harris and Mule Suttles' bat dropped another fly ball into the accurate hands of Harris. This sounded taps for the West, because from then on Sir Satchel was the master of the situation.

Paige sustained the shutout and finally saw his team win the game rather undramatically when Jud Wilson singled home Cool Papa Bell in the eighth inning. The game was all pitching, all Satchel, as the legendary John Henry Lloyd, the finest black performer anywhere of decades before, commented, "I told you last year, you can't beat unbeatable pitching."

For his part, Josh drilled a double and a single, but he was again outhit by Mule Suttles. The Mule got three hits, one a triple in the fourth inning which threatened to break up the game. Suttles attempted to score from third on a sacrifice fly as Jimmie Crutchfield in right cranked up everything he had in his five-foot, eight-inch body and rifled the ball on a line to the plate. Gibson caught it on the fly and, without moving, put the tag on the lumbering Suttles. It was an incredible play, and the crowd jumped to its feet in applause.

No All-Star game was to be as scintillating as the 1935 contest, a game that was played by more players from different teams than the previous games. Held on August 11, again in front of 25,000 fans, the contest embodied the essence of Negro baseball: the attraction that it had for black people, and why, because of the game's proportions, it became one of the proudest, most prized moments of the segregated game.

One change in the 1935 game was a team selection which put the Crawford and Gray All-Stars on the West squad. That grouped Gibson, Charleston, Bell, and other Easterners with the best of the Chicago American Giants—Alex "Double Duty" Radcliffe, Teddy Trent, and the big slugger, Mule Suttles. For once, Josh and Mule, two would-be "black Babe Ruths," were on the same team.

The amazing results are best relived through the eyes of William G. Nunn, a young *Courier* sportswriter and the official scorer for the game.

PRESS BOX, COMISKEY PARK, Aug. 11—"For the West, Mule Suttles at bat!"

That's the resonant voice of the announcer, speaking through the new public address system of the park.

"T-H-E M-U-L-E!"

Reverberating through the reaches of this historic ballpark and bounding and rebounding through the packed stands comes the chant of some 25,000 frenzied spectators.

They're yelling for blood! They're yelling for their idol, the bronzed Babe Ruth of colored baseball to come through.

It's more than a call! It's a chant! It's a prayer! Surely, that superb slugger out there, pitting his eyes against the blinding speed-ball of one of the greatest all-around ballplayers ever to tear up turf with pitching spikes, has heard the call! But let us show you the picture in its entirety.

Prior to the eleventh inning of the East-West classic, the East, underdogs of the game, had bared their fangs early to grip a lead only to see it melt into nothingness in the latter innings of the contest.

Through the ninth, the two teams had battled to a 4-4 stalemate. Into the tenth they had gone, and it was here that the East had made its "gesture supreme." Four times they had crossed the plate, to apparently pack the game away on ice.

And then, as in an Horatio Alger "hero book," the East, with their backs to the wall, had scored four runs in their half of the tenth to even things up again, 8-8.

Throughout the first half of the eleventh, the West had held the East scoreless. There were no more innings on the scorebook, and we'd gone over to another page.

Then came the last half of the eleventh.

Cool Papa Bell had worked Dihigo, who had come out of centerfield to pitch for the East, into a hole and had strolled to first base. Hughes went out, Dihigo to Dandridge on a perfect sacrifice as Bell blurred the other way scooting to the mid-way station.

Chester Williams was called out on strikes after vehemently insisting that one of Dihigo's blazing speedballs had hit him.

Josh Gibson, catching for the West, and who had connected for two doubles and two singles in five trips to the plate, was purposely shunted.

And that's the picture as the announcer's voice, rather hoarse from detailing eleven innings of superb competition, announced: "For the West, Suttles at bat."

Dihigo, his uniform dripping with perspiration, wiped the sweat out of his eyes, and shot a fast ball across the plate. Ball one, said Umpire Craig.

Again, came that blinding fastball, letter high and splitting the plate. And the count was one and one.

Suttles stepped out of the batter's box, dried his sweating palms in the dust around home plate, tugged on his cap, and moved back into position. He looked dangerous as he wangled his big, black club around. But so did Dihigo, who was giving his all.

Once again came that smooth motion, that reflex action of the arm, and then!—a blur seeming to catapult towards the plate.

Suttles threw his mighty body into motion. His foot moved forward. His huge shoulder muscles bunched. Came a swish through the air, a crack as of a rifle, and like a projectile hurled from a cannon, the ball started its meteoric flight. On a line it went. It was headed towards right center. Bell and Gibson were away with the crack of the bat. But so was Arnold, centerfielder of the East team and Oms, dependable and dangerous Cuban star, who patroled the right garden. No one thought the ball could carry to the stands.

Headed as it was, it took a drive of better than 450 feet to clear the fence.

The ball continued on its course and the packed stands rose to their feet. Was it going to be caught?! Was it going to hit the stands?!

No, folks! That ball, ticketed by Mule Suttles, CLEARED the distant fence in far away right center, landing 475 feet from home plate. It was a herculean swat. One of the greatest in baseball. As cheering momentarily hushed in the greatest tribute an athlete can ever receive, we in the press box heard it strike the back of a seat with a resounding thud, and then go bounding merrily on its way.

And then . . . pandemonium broke loose. Suttles completed his trip home, the third-base line filled with playmates anxious to draw him to their breasts. Over the stands came a surging mass of humanity.

7

Holdouts and Jumpers

When Josh first caught for the Homestead Grays that July day in 1930, he, like any black kid in Pittsburgh at the time, would gladly have played for nothing. In fact, he was doing just that until Cum Posey got around to negotiating a salary for the remainder of the season. Yet it didn't take long for Josh and the rest of the players to get over the flattery they felt at being asked to play with the best. They were playing ball in the Depression—Josh as a pro knew few other times—and that meant a meager, impoverished existence in which many teams folded, players were often not paid at all, revenues came in after passing the hat, and established teams asked their stars to accept rock-bottom salaries or a percentage of the gate.

As rough as it was, Josh began to realize as the years passed that he was a valuable property even in a buyers' market. He was a polished star in the league and in exhibitions, a slugger whose blasts received as much publicity as the rest of the team combined, with the exception of Satchel Paige. Josh didn't have to search for an estimate of his worth as a ballplayer, for even though the Negro leagues never awarded most-valuable-player awards, he quickly knew he was one of the very best.

Take the 1933 season. Official league records were not kept, or they were done so haphazardly that no reliable figures emerged. The Crawfords as a team, however, kept track of their totals. For the '33 season, Josh played 137 games, missing only a dozen or so. He batted 512 times, collected a fantastic 239 hits,

96

and batted .467, a total that led the team by almost 100 percentage points. Oscar Charleston batted .374, and Ted Page, Cool Papa Bell, and Bill Perkins all hit around .360. Josh led the team in triples, home runs (with 55), and was second only to Bell and Charleston in runs scored.

The figures mean little overall because the competition was so varied, but they do tell a lot about how Josh performed compared with his teammates, and at a time when the Pittsburgh Crawfords were among the top teams, if not *the* top, in Negro baseball. He was a complete ball player; his statistics did not lie. He did not rely on an unforgettable home run to smooth over days of unproductive hitting, for he was seldom unproductive.

With such a record, it was no surprise that Josh became sensitive about the kind of money he was making. So many black ballplayers looked upon their existence during the Depression, and the fact that average salaries ran about $125 a month, with a benign sense of acceptance. It was better than sweeping or working the railroad, where wages amounted to $60 to $75 a month. Josh had pushed his salary to the $250-to $400-a-month range by the mid-1930s, and nobody denied that he was worth every penny of it. Only Satchel Paige was getting more, not necessarily with his salary, but usually because he made extra money when he was loaned out to other teams for exhibitions. Josh never enjoyed such arrangements.

He could have used them for his expenses at the time were significant. Besides providing support for his two children, Josh was living with a Pittsburgh woman named Hattie. She was an older woman, and one who had little to do with the wives of other players. In fact, many of them wondered about the arrangement, for Hattie seldom attended Josh's games and seemed to them to be jealous of his success and fame. She kept to herself, worked as a housekeeper, and when she was seen in public with Josh, she seemed to have an almost stifling effect on his general good nature. Still, the two of them stayed together in what most of Josh's teammates knew to be a common-law marriage.

With such added responsibilities, Josh paid more attention to money. He never showed it on the field or with his teammates, but he had become a tenacious negotiator at contract time. That became necessary, for although Greenlee had a reputation for treating his players well on and off the field, even he could not buck his team's Depression-era receipts. He gave his players, including Josh, the going rates and fought them for those.

Just as Josh was beginning to realize his earning power, his psychological nemesis, Babe Ruth, was losing his. The 1930s were the beginning of the end for Ruth, and after 1932 he saw his salary chopped each year until he retired. Even the Yankees' Col. Jacob Ruppert couldn't meet Ruth's $80,000 salary with what the Depression was doing to his gate, and in 1933 he paid Ruth only $52,000. In 1934, that went down to $35,000. Still, even that was an awesome sum when compared to the money Josh and his teammates were making.

The reason, in some minds, was something other than the economic hard times. To Johnny Drew, black owner of the Philadelphia Hilldale team, it had a lot to do with blacks and black owners selling their game short. In 1933, Drew, who admitted that he was a wealthy man and was not in baseball to make money, said that black ballplayers had not been given the respect and the money due them. "For him [the black ballplayer] there has never been any future, nobody has ever thought of making it possible for him to earn a salary of five thousand dollars a year. He has been exploited and bamboozled by the very men for whom he made fortunes in the past," Drew declared.

He maintained that black baseball had to be put on a "business basis," and that even though owners were cutting salaries in 1933, it was being done in order to put the finances of the leagues back in shape. What was also needed was cooperation from fans.

"Negro fans do not have the proper sense of values . . . last year I was criticized for having dollar box seats and they told me that was too much to charge for a colored team. When we played the white All Stars up at the Phillies' park I saw at least eight hundred Negro fans sitting in the grandstand seats which cost them a dollar. Among them were many who had refused to pay a dollar at Hilldale," Drew said.

Drew's argument made sense, but it did little to overcome resistance to admission prices at the ball parks—black and white, but particularly black—during the Depression. Drew, for his part, never followed through with his liberal theories to the point where he ever offered top stars like Gibson and Paige the salaries which would have given them the "respect" known to major-league stars. Drew also said he was certain blacks would be in the major leagues in "five or ten years," another of his predictions that never really came close.

An event which had more effect on black ballplayers and the money they were making was the fuss Babe Ruth put up when his salary was cut. Every sports page detailed Ruth's contract bickering, and every player, black and white, brought Babe's arguments with him to his own bargaining table. Ruth, however, was an overwhelming exception to the general level of major-league salaries. In 1927, the rest of the Yankees, players who made up a team regarded as one of the best in baseball, made considerably less money than the Babe. Herb Pennock made $17,500, Joe Dugan and Waite Hoyt $12,000, Lou Gehrig $8,000, and pitcher Wilcy Moore, who won nineteen and lost seven, received only $3,000. Against those figures, the salaries of Gibson and Paige, while paltry, were not so disproportionate as baseball historians through the years have led fans to believe. The fact is that the average salary of the black player was approximately one-quarter that of his major-league counterpart and about equal to that of minor-league ball players—Frank McCormick, for example, signed with the Cincinnati Reds in 1934 for $100 a month—and then only when the black ballplayer was receiving any salary at all. Gibson and Paige, as overwhelming star attractions, weren't even making what the journeyman major-league ballplayer could expect.

There were other theories about Ruth's impact on the game. Al Monroe of the Chicago *Defender* said Ruth was responsible for bringing about an era of high salaries in baseball, and that it was the big money, not racism, that kept blacks out of organized ball. White people were not about to share the wealth, Monroe claimed. Ruth's retirement, Monroe added, would change things. Purses would come down as Ruth's had in his last few years, and with them would tumble the color bar.

That theory went the way of so much other wishful thinking concerning the major-league race barrier. The reality of high salaries did not fade, especially as far as Josh was concerned. By 1936, after four years with the Crawfords, he was no longer a soft touch for an unsigned contract. He also chafed under the publicity Satchel Paige continued to generate. Greenlee, in his white shirt and suspenders, was hard-pressed to meet Josh's price or to solve the slugger's natural resentment of Paige. In fact, by the end of the season, Greenlee realized he might be unable to keep Josh from jumping the Crawfords.

By the end of the 1936 season, the Crawfords were not the same organization they had been for the preceding five seasons. Greenlee through the years had tasted success and put himself and his team atop the Negro baseball world. They had posed each year in front of the stadium with Gus's name on it, before the sleek buses which traveled all over the country, in the well-tailored uniforms with "Crawfords" or just the six-inch letter "P" across the front. He had watched them crisscross the country to win big games and attract tremendous crowds to major-league parks or to sandlot fields; he had seen them dominate the East-West All Star games at Comiskey Park. All of it was a pleasure to the outgoing, aggressive owner, but none of it made him any money.

Though the Crawfords had been synonymous with the best in

the game since 1932, their lineup of Bell, Crutchfield, Page, Charleston, Gibson, Johnson, and Paige a dream of a scorecard, the green bus and the flashy Crawford uniforms a carnival of touring delights—the pride, the electricity, the flash—the team still failed to beat the depressed times. At no time in the Crawford heyday from 1932 through 1937 did the operation turn a profit. Such was the reality of Negro baseball and the Great Depression.

By 1937 Gus had also began to feel the pinch in the rackets back in Pittsburgh. His numbers games were no longer immune to police vice squads. Reports held that his games were raided repeatedly on the strength of tips supplied to police by an employee at the Crawford Grille. Whatever the reason, Gus began to economize and look for ways to cut corners on team expenses.

Greenlee's problems with Gibson began in January of that year. While Josh was still down in Puerto Rico playing winter ball, the Crawfords announced that a contract dispute had arisen. The owner of an Eastern club, not publicly identified but actually Edward Bolden of the Philadelphia Stars, had offered Josh a high salary to be player-manager of the club. Posey's Homestead Grays also wanted him and had offered $2,500 and two players for Josh and the aging but still superb third baseman Judy Johnson. (The local press ballyhooed the trade by calling it the "Punch 'n' Judy Show," with Josh the obvious "punch" behind the offer.)

Although laughable by most standards, the $2,500 and two players, later revealed to be catcher Pepper Bassett and infielder Henry Spearman, was a serious offer, even for players of the caliber of Gibson and Johnson. Judy, however, was so offended by the trade attempt that he announced his retirement. (He later reconsidered, and finally retired after the 1938 season.) Josh wasn't heard from until late February when he returned north, and then he decided to hold out until the best offer came in.

Such a position wasn't like him, and the press and team

owners did not really know how to respond. He had always been accessible, open, and amenable to any agreement club owners drew up for him. Now, though he was only twenty-five, he was nobody's patsy at the negotiating table. All the games, the days on the road, and the hundreds of base hits had made him a veteran of more things than just what happened on the field.

The *Courier* reported his holdout with a conspicuous amount of reproach. "Even the pinochle figures which Gibson has mentioned in connection with his salary have thrown no light on his intentions for 1937," the paper said.

John L. Clark, Greenlee's secretary and spokesman, was even more blunt. For the first time, the Crawfords as an organization openly criticized their prized slugger. "The most aggravating holdout in the Negro National League happens to be none other than Josh Gibson, first-string receiver for the Pittsburgh Crawfords," Clark wrote. He went on to say that Josh's salary demand was not unreasonable, but that a "complex temperament had been developing in the past year." What he really meant was that Josh was sick of playing for nothing.

Clark, with the support of Greenlee, and oddly, that of Cum Posey and Rufus Jackson of the Grays, also said that problems with Josh had been aggravated by offers from other owners. The attitude was typical of owners, black and white, almost throughout the history of baseball. What they wanted was a bargaining straitjacket around each player, a reserve clause which would keep players from the free market and make them duty-bound to their present owners. Posey wrote, "There should be a penalty for league owners who deal with other league owners' players, offering larger salaries and making the players dissatisfied." Ballplayers black or white, such reasoning went, were not part of a common labor market, but indentured employees.

Josh, for his part, did not relent on his demand for what Clark called a "stunning" salary figure. He said to Greenlee that he could get it from the unnamed Eastern club and that he would if the Crawfords didn't match the offer. Clark, always with the last word in the press, argued that Gibson each year had "dickered" for more money from the Crawfords, and that in return he has "showed improvement each season."

What followed, in a column that black baseball fans in Pittsburgh and around the country read to a word, was a disparaging assessment of Gibson's abilities which was intended to lessen his worth in the eyes of the public and, Clark and Greenlee hoped, in Josh's own eyes.

Gibson, in Clark's estimation, was a good hitter who stroked the ball hard and often. He was

alert and has a way of getting the best a pitcher has to offer. Strangely, he is one of the best runners to be found anywhere.

He is an asset to any club. But not the kind of asset more colorful and less capable players might be. With all of his ability, he has not developed that *it* which pulls the cash customers through the turnstiles . . . although he has been publicized as much as Satchel Paige.

With this shortcoming charged against him, the complex which has engrossed him, and the inclination to play two ends against the middle, it is likely that Greenlee will sell or trade Gibson to the highest bidder.

It sounded good in the *Courier*, but nobody believed it for a minute. Pittsburgh fans saw salary wrangling for what it was, and also realized the attraction Josh was, even if Greenlee didn't want to meet his salary. The Pittsburgh fans, oddly enough, ended up with winners, for the deal went through with the Grays for Bassett and Spearman and $2,500. Josh, though a "perpetual holdout" in the eyes of a *Courier* sportswriter, would make the Grays formidable once again. The trade was called "the biggest player deal in the history of Negro baseball," the sum of money an offer lower only than the $5,000 sum offered to Satchel Paige in an unsuccessful bid in 1934 by the Newark Eagles.

Gibson accepted the terms of his new bosses and reported for Gray spring training in Jacksonville, Florida, that April. He even proceeded to homer twice against the Miami Clowns in an exhibition. The Crawfords, with Greenlee not quite ready to

abandon his baseball fortunes, attempted to bolster the reputation of Pepper Bassett, their new catcher. Bassett had caught
some exhibitions in a rocking chair, and in an obvious ploy to
make Crawford fans forget their old catcher, Greenlee made a
multicolored rocking chair for Bassett to sit in in pickup games
and to use to warm up pitchers before league games. He also
called Bassett's arm the greatest in baseball, saying that he "can
knock a gnat off a dwarf's ear at 100 yards." Along with Satchel,
Greenlee believed, such a catcher would be a big drawing card, a
bigger one, it was hoped, than the previous year's battery.

But few Crawford fans were willing to downgrade Josh or to
bury him beneath new talent. In a *Courier* interview shortly
after the trade, Negro-league umpire John Craig said that Josh
had the greatest arm by far of any catcher in the league. Biz
Mackey, Craig felt, was the receiver with the best all-around
ability, but as far as a wing was concerned, nobody—not even
Pepper Bassett in a rocking chair or out of it—could outgun
Josh.

The trade controversy appeared solved, however, and by April
the owners and fans prepared for the new season, no matter who
was playing for what team. But a development even more
threatening than player holdouts was brewing behind the scenes,
and it involved players from every major black team.

Because hard times had cut into the salaries of the biggest
stars, club owners in Cuba and Puerto Rico were increasingly
able to lure them south for the summer season. The issue was
money, and if enough of it could be flashed in front of stars like
Paige, Gibson, and Bell, the foreign owners believed that even
these players would forsake their traditional American summer
schedules.

Two Cuban players, Martin Dihigo and Lazaro Salazar,
acted as agents for foreign owners. They were excellent judges of
talent, for Dihigo, as pitcher for the New York Cubans, was, in
the minds of many observers, one of Negro baseball's top

performers. In a matter of weeks, through March and April of 1937, the two men performed what was labeled by league owners as a "Cuban raid" on American players. They signed Clarence "Spoony" Palm, a catcher for the New York Black Yankees, Bill Perkins of the Crawfords, and the Craws' new outfielder, Thad Christopher. They also signed Henry Spearman and David "Showboat" Thomas of the Cubans.

With such talent going south, Greenlee and other league owners decided to take legal action. They hired attorneys to sue the jumping players and also to get a court injunction against Dihigo and Salazar. Meanwhile, they were shortchanging their own ballplayers whenever they had the chance. The Crawfords were training down in New Orleans, and Greenlee told them that they had to pay their own expenses, something previous club budgets had always taken care of.

Satchel Paige, though as unreliable as ever, remained with the Crawfords despite Greenlee's tightening wallet. But even he could not avoid agents working for yet another South American baseball mogul. Though they had never played there, black players were aware of the spirited baseball competition down in the Dominican Republic. Baseball in that country, as in Puerto Rico, Cuba, and Mexico, permeated most aspects of the culture, even politics, for strong teams from their respective cities made politicians look equally strong. It was simply bad form to be adroit in cigar-smoke-filled rooms but inept on the diamond, and politicians, especially those who personally sponsored teams, took pains to stock their clubs with talent.

One of these baseball politicos was Rafael Trujillo, the young president of the country who had come to power in 1930 through a military coup. His hold on the country was a shaky one, and in early 1937 his baseball team was weak. To remedy that, he sent his scouts all over South American countries signing up ballplayers, but the one he wanted the most was the gangling fireballer of the Pittsburgh Crawfords. Trujillo's men approached Paige, but he resisted them for a variety of reasons, one of which was the fact that he had gotten into considerable trouble with Greenlee and the rest of the league with his perpetual jumping to places such as Bismarck, North Dakota. As Cool Papa Bell tells the story, Trujillo's men followed Paige all over and finally cornered him outside his New Orleans hotel. Satchel dodged them and drove off, but they finally blocked his car and confronted him with an offer he couldn't refuse.

Paige's jump, as expected, enraged league officials up north. *Courier* sportswriter Chester Washington said Paige should be barred from baseball for good, for he was "as undependable as a pair of second-hand suspenders." Greenlee added that Paige, like the players who had signed with Dihigo and Salazar earlier, were "killing the goose that laid the golden egg." Threats followed, including more legal action, and Greenlee announced that no matter what it took to get jumping players back in line, "these men must realize that the league is far larger and more powerful than they are."

But the feel of their empty pockets made more of an impact on league players than did Greenlee's wrath. Paige found that his new team in Santo Domingo was pretty bad—in fact, dead last in the standings. He cabled back to the States for some of his teammates. The man he contacted was Cool Papa Bell. Bell had a reputation for dependability and straight dealings as a ballplayer and a businessman, and Satchel knew that if he could convince Bell to come, other Crawfords would follow. He was authorized to offer $800 a man for six weeks, travel and expenses included.

"Satchel," Cool Papa responded, "they treatin' us so bad here we'll come down. But make it a thousand and we'll stay eight weeks."

The offer was okayed, even to the point of paying Bell and the others half of the money up front. Arrangements were made to meet Dominican representatives in Miami. Bell showed up with teammates Harry Williams, Leroy Matlock, and Sammy Bankhead. They were met as arranged at the Miami airport, and over dinner in a restaurant, the foreigners handed each player $500 in cash, as much money as some of them saw in three months of playing for the Crawfords. A short time later, they were in Santo Domingo, being greeted by the smiling rogue, Paige.

Paige also wanted Josh down there, and he was authorized to offer $2,200 for seven weeks of ballplaying. Josh didn't jump with Bell and the others since he was playing with the Grays at the time. Yet there was little indecision on his part, and he notified Cum Posey of his intentions. Posey, no doubt, did not like losing his star catcher for even a year, and he resented the jumping of Bell and the other Craws—he said at the time that "there have been no baseball players in our history of colored baseball who have been more petted and pampered than were those of the Crawford players and Gus Greenlee"—but he realized that he didn't have much choice with Gibson. Rather than alienate him, he announced that Josh had received the okay of management before he went south. However reluctant that "okay" may have been, Josh, at the beginning of June, was on the "Beeline" train to Miami, then a plane to Santo Domingo.

He joined Paige and the other Craws to make up the nucleus of Trujillo's squad in San Pedro de Macoris, a small town about forty miles from Santo Domingo. A lot of stories have evolved from the competition there, the most exaggerated saying that the Americans were told that they had to win or else, and that "or else" meant a firing squad. Actually, no such ultimatum was given, even though players were restricted to their hotel in San Pedro when they weren't playing and were guarded there around the clock.

The games were politically charged affairs, with hosts of government officials in attendance and a spattering of disciplined uniformed troops in the crowd. The soldiers carried rifles with bayonets that glittered in the sunlight, and whenever the American players gazed into the stands, they could not help but spot the glint of steel. As the games progressed, the Trujillo team dominated its competition, the most serious challenge coming from a team from Santiago, and on the final day clinched the championship. Trujillo was thus saved the embarrassment of a losing team, and stayed in office. The Crawfords were later told, in what was the closest thing to an ultimatum, that if they had not won and Trujillo's forces had been overthrown, the ballplayers probably would not have gotten out of the country alive.

Josh stayed there his seven weeks, collected his $2,200, and by mid-July was back in Pittsburgh playing for the Grays. It had been well worth his while, for he was back playing for the best team in Negro baseball, and Cum Posey, in his inimitable way of forgetting past sins in favor of present favors, touted his catcher as "the greatest player in the history of Negro baseball."

Paige, Bell, and the other renegade Crawfords returned to the States complete with their Trujillo uniforms. They signed up a few additional players and barnstormed throughout the Midwest for a promoter named Ray Doan, calling themselves the "Trujillo All-Stars," or the "Santo Domingo Negro Stars." They, too, had done well in Central America, even if they did bear the brunt of the Negro-league owners' wrath upon their return. They were barred from the annual East-West All-Star game in Chicago. Cum Posey even complained that they should somehow be prohibited from barnstorming. They were not, however, and even proceeded to win the Denver *Post* Tournament. Finally, in a startling business move, but one common in the opportunistic world of Negro baseball, Crawford business manager John L. Clark began to book exhibition games for them in the Pittsburgh area. Such developments provided the jumpers with little worry of getting back on Negro-league teams, for they were among the best of its players. Satchel was Satchel, and for every owner who attempted to honor an unofficial blackball edict against them, another was more than eager to sign them and reap the rewards.

The 1937 season saw Greenlee and his Crawfords with but a semblance of the lineup that had been so formidable since 1932. Josh was on the Grays; Ted Page had torn the cartilage in his knee and retired after the 1935 season; Crutchfield had gone to the Newark Eagles; Bell had gone down to Mexico. Satchel finished out with the Trujillo All-Stars, and few expected him to get back to terms with the Crawfords. That turned out to be the case, for at the start of the following year he became embroiled in a salary dispute after Greenlee had offered him $450 a month. He told Gus, "I wouldn't throw ice cubes for that kind of money," and soon he was sold to Abe and Effa Manley's Newark Eagles.

Only Oscar Charleston and a few veteran infielders remained with the Crawfords, but Charleston was well into his forties, overweight, nasty—he repeatedly got into wild fistfights with players and umpires—and not the exquisite athlete he had been ten years before. The Craws managed to get only three men in the East-West All-Star game. They were infielder Chester Williams, pitcher Barney Morris, and Pepper Bassett, Gibson's successor behind the plate. Bassett, in fact, had a superb year and hit .444, making the hulking 230-pound catcher a remarkable replacement for Josh. *Courier* sportswriters even went so far as to say that Pepper's performance might make the Craws "all but forget about Josh next season."

Yet Bassett was the lone bright spot in an otherwise dismal season for the once-proud Crawfords. They finished fifth out of six teams in the league's first half, winning eleven and losing sixteen games. In their traditional Fourth of July series with the Grays, the Craws lost three straight. But perhaps most important, the Crawfords seemed to lose the image of a winner, the flash of Negro baseball's classiest team. *Courier* columnist Washington said the team fell from the best-publicized team to the worst: "In past years whenever the Crawfords invaded the East, Midwest, or any other section of the country, the publicity buildup which preceded them made the coming of the club the talk of the town. It was like the coming of the circus." But not in 1937, when the life and the spirit and the pizzazz of the team seemed to have gone the way of its departed superstars.

Club secretary John Clark reacted bitterly to Washington's criticisms, partly because it had been Clark, a widely read newspaper writer and public-relations man for Greenlee, who had been responsible for the change. He insisted that in the years since 1932 it had been the Crawfords who had carried all of Negro baseball, who had put money and spirit and enthusiasm into a sagging enterprise. "Games with the Crawfords were publicized all over the nation. News was sent to every black paper," he wrote, as if to confirm Washington's charge. "The change occurred not because of the Crawfords' management, but because of the players who had forsaken the club and cast their lot with foreigners." And in a final swipe at Satchel, Josh, Bell, Bankhead, and the others who had left the team and, in Clark's mind, forsaken the franchise, Clark wrote, "This has convinced me that publicizing colored players is a thankless job."

The same kind of disillusionment affected Greenlee, and by the end of the season his enthusiasm for organized baseball had cooled. He still prized the power he had in the Negro leagues, and he continued to feud with other owners over player raids and league procedures. He was irked in September when a World Series was set up between Homestead and the Kansas City Monarchs and done so without his authority. He accused club owners such as Posey, Rufus Jackson, and the Manleys of being interested "only in themselves and their own selfish motives." The charge was not a new one, nor was Greenlee's lack of patience with league conditions. It would be a matter of time and a combination of other reverses before Gus closed up his Crawford shop and called it quits in baseball.

For Josh, however, the 1937 season had been a good one in all ways. Even with his seven-week stay in Santo Domingo, he hit sixty-two home runs for the Grays during their season. At the close of it, he went to Texas with a team of Negro-league players and competed in a tournament in Houston. From there, he went on to winter ball in Puerto Rico.

Back in Pittsburgh, Cum Posey filled the off-season *Courier* with glowing adjectives about his catcher. "The best we can do is to say Josh Gibson is the best baseball player, white or colored, that we have seen in all our years of following baseball," Posey wrote. He lamented the fact that Josh wasn't in the majors and said that in the face of such an injustice, "all personal liberty cases become a mockery."

Posey's lament was an incessant but painfully appropriate reality within the baseball world, both black and white, a criticism which became even more poignant when applied at the team level. Had the Pittsburgh Pirates, for example, a team which came close to taking the National League pennant in 1937, decided to sign not just a Gibson or a Paige but a *cluster* of top black stars—six or seven of the best—the entire Pirate franchise would have been transformed.

And most of baseball knew it. During the winter meetings of baseball club owners in Chicago that year, Chester Washington of the *Courier* sent a telegram to Pirate manager Pie Traynor.

PIE TRAYNOR. PITTSBURGH PIRATES. CONGRESS HOTEL. KNOW YOUR CLUB NEEDS PLAY-ERS STOP HAVE ANSWERS TO YOUR PRAYERS RIGHT HERE IN PITTSBURGH STOP JOSH GIBSON CATCHER B. LEONARD 1B AND RAY BROWN PITCHER OF HOMESTEAD GRAYS AND S. PAIGE PITCHER COOL PAPA BELL OF PITTSBURGH CRAWFORDS ALL AVAILABLE AT REASON-ABLE FIGURES STOP WOULD MAKE PIRATES FORMIDABLE PENNANT CONTENDERS STOP WHAT IS YOUR ATTITUDE? WIRE ANSWER.

But Washington, and all of Negro baseball, received no reply. The Pirates finished the 1938 season in second place, two games behind the Chicago Cubs. And baseball historians, people whose minds thrive on speculation and hypothesis—the endless "what-if" propositions which have filled the game since its inception—can only shake their heads in wonderment at the idea of a 1938 Pittsburgh Pirate roster with that kind of black talent.

Without it, the Pirates and Pittsburgh waited twenty-two more years before they finally made it to the top.

8

The Absentee Star

In the spring of 1938, just back from the winter leagues in Cuba, Josh was about to become part of the resurgence of his old nemesis, the Homestead Grays. The Crawfords and Gus Greenlee were still in business, but minus the initiative to resign the ballplayers he once had and rebuild the team. The impending loss of Satchel Paige ensured the Crawford demise. The rest of the league, as usual, also suffered from unstable organization and fiscal troubles, and the weakness of its parts made the league as a whole a dubious prospect. Journalists wrote that Negro baseball was in need of another Rube Foster, an iron-fisted personality who could dictate policy and meld a league together. Only Cum Posey came close to such a description, but he did not have the combination of power and politics to run the league as Foster had in the 1920s, even if Cum was a consistently strong force within it.

Posey, however, with the help of his brother Seward and co-owners such as Rufus Jackson and others, was quite able to keep the Grays together as a team and as an organization. He remained a peerless judge of talent, just as he had been for fifteen years, and consistently stocked the Grays with solid ballplayers in all positions. His teams earned the appellation "the New York Yankees of Negro baseball," especially in the late 1930s when Gibson teamed with first baseman Buck Leonard, the stocky, bull-necked left-hander from Rocky

Mount, North Carolina, to form a tandem every bit as awesome as that of Ruth and Gehrig.

For his part, in 1938, Josh at twenty-seven was in the prime of his career, a veteran of every kind of competition, a player with supreme confidence to complement his power and his savvy. With contract problems settled for the year, and the psychological competition of Satchel Paige somewhat removed, Josh was easygoing and a pleasure to manage. He was a simple, gregarious, spirited kid who saw nothing much to his life outside the game of baseball.

In April 1938 he signed his Gray contract and stayed for an interview with Cum Posey. It was totally shoptalk, revealing little about Josh except his knowledge of the game and the competition. And Posey, a cunning, educated man who nevertheless seldom let his attention stray from the pale of athletics, was content to keep the conversation completely between the baselines.

POSEY: How does colored baseball at the present time compare with colored baseball at the time you broke in during 1930?

GIBSON: It is better now. We have a league now which we consider well organized. I feel as though I have something to play for now, besides just making a payday.

POSEY: What did you consider your best year?

GIBSON: 1931.

POSEY: What pitcher had best control of any pitcher you ever caught?

GIBSON: Smokey Joe Williams.

POSEY: Who was the smartest pitcher?

GIBSON: Two of them. Sam Streeter and W. Bell.

POSEY: What pitcher was the best at holding men on base?

GIBSON: Nick Stanley. I caught him in Puerto Rico.

POSEY: What park do you prefer to play in of all parks?

GIBSON: Polo Grounds of New York.

POSEY: No use asking you why as I know it is on account of the short left-field stands.

GIBSON: Right field, too.

POSEY: What was the hardest hit ball you ever hit?

GIBSON: Last year at Farmers [East Orange, New Jersey], and in 1930 at Yankee Stadium.

POSEY: How far did you hit them?

GIBSON: At Farmers I hit the ball over the left-field fence and over a two-story station outside the park. At Yankee Stadium I hit the ball on a line into the bullpen in deep left field.

Then Posey proceeded to ask Josh who he thought was best at each position. Josh, without elaborating, replied each time with a single name. Posey then changed the line of questions.

POSEY: Where do white fans appear to appreciate colored baseball the most?

GIBSON: Dexter Park, Brooklyn; Farmers, East Orange, New Jersey; Belman, Phillipsburg, New Jersey; and in Philadelphia.

POSEY: Have you played against many major-league players?

GIBSON: Too many to remember—Hornsby, Foxx, Dean brothers, Pepper Martin, Whitehead, Hack Wilson, Manush, Ted Lyons.

POSEY: Did you ever hit a home run off Dizzy Dean?

GIBSON: Yes, in York, P.A.

POSEY: How did you bat in Cuba the past winter?

GIBSON: I hit .401.

POSEY: I guess that's all, Josh.

GIBSON: No, that's not all. Why don't you ask me how I think I will come out when I face Satchel Paige this year?

POSEY: That's interesting to everybody. Satch against Josh. What do you figure?

GIBSON: I look to get an even break, two out of four. One thousand in a pinch, providing Charleston don't say, "Put him on."

And that was that. Josh left for San Antonio, Texas, to train with the Grays and immediately started pounding the ball. He played third base briefly to strengthen the team's infield. By May he was back behind the plate, and the Grays were romping past their competition. In late June they were safely in first place, and sportswriters were again comparing the team to the best clubs in the history of Negro baseball. When the first half of the league's season ended, the Grays record stood at 26-6. Josh and Buck Leonard paced the team, and each led the voting by wide margins for the East-West game.

The 1938 season was not so easy for most other Negro teams. All were losing money; the league was hard-pressed to put together a complete schedule. The Crawfords doggedly stayed together despite a young, largely unknown roster and a meager following. With Oscar Charleston pushing them, the Craws managed to win fourteen games and lose fourteen in the first half of the season. With Gus Greenlee's negligible interest in the team, it was remarkable that it still played at all.

Greenlee's financial reverses continued to mount as 1938 progressed. His numbers rackets were not generating the capital they once had, even though they remained a daily routine in Pittsburgh's black areas. His other athletic enterprise, boxing and the management of light-heavyweight John H. Lewis, also brought heavy losses. A scheduled Lewis bout with "Two-Ton" Tony Galento, a bulbous heavyweight who had lost to Joe Louis, was lavishly publicized, but just prior to the fight Galento became sick and pulled out of the match. It was never re-scheduled, and after all expenses were totaled, the cancellation reportedly cost Greenlee $300,000.

Such a setback was almost too much for the powerful, garrulous Greenlee. Debts and government tax claims followed, and by December 1938, Gus had little alternative but to sacrifice the weakest parts of his holding. That meant the Crawfords, the source of much pride and glory but a constant financial drain. It also meant the sacrifice of the stadium they played in. On the tenth of the month, wreckers showed up at Greenlee Field and began to dismantle it. Only six years after it had been constructed at a cost of $125,000, after it had been cited as the flagship of Greenlee's sparkling baseball endeavors and celebrated as one of the few black-owned stadiums in the country, the ball park was demolished and the land sold. It was an event which stung Negro baseball, and most observers agreed that the game was at its lowest point since 1932, the very year Greenlee had jumped into the game and given it an impressive, spirited design.

Gus had left only his Crawford Grille on Wylie Avenue, and it remained the top spot for athletes and politicians and gamblers and anyone who was anyone in black Pittsburgh. He paid close attention to it at that time in order to ensure its existence, for with debts assaulting him on all sides, the Grille came into doubt. Things were not helped by a John H. Lewis fight with Joe Louis the following January. Joe knocked out John Henry in one minute ten seconds of the first round. A month later, Greenlee threw in another towel and resigned as president of the Negro National League. His baseball fortunes were finished, and he said in parting that what was needed to help the league out of its present problems was "new blood." He had lost enough of his with the Craws.

Organized Negro baseball in early 1939 faced more problems than the loss of Greenlee and the Crawfords. The lure of foreign teams again damaged the league's stature in more devastating ways than the annual bath of red ink. Team resources were so depressed at the time that wages had become laughably low, so much so that they provided foreign baseball interests with a golden opportunity to entice American stars with lucrative year-round contracts.

In early 1939, Mexican and Venezuelan owners, most of them wielding hefty bankrolls and enjoying government backing, approached Negro-league stars with offers as high as $2,200 to $4,000 for the summer season. That was double—in some cases, triple and quadruple—the money offered by American owners. And players like Gibson, Sam Bankhead, Cool Papa Bell, Raymond Brown, and others, after playing in Cuba until January, then moving to Puerto Rico, were sorely tempted to accept foreign contracts even though they preferred to play up north and knew they would earn the ire of the owners and the fans if they did not.

As spring approached, and grumblings over players jumping to foreign countries surfaced repeatedly in black newspapers, more and more established stars decided to opt for the money and stay south. Cool Papa Bell stayed on in the Mexican league, as did many black players, including the popular Cuban Martin Dihigo, Willie Wells, and the awesome Chicago American Giant right-hander, Chet Brewer.

Yet in May of that year, the Grays proudly announced that Josh had returned from Puerto Rico and was in spring training with the Grays. It was the same Josh who by that time was getting impressive notice from white sportswriters. Shirley Povich of the Washington *Post* wrote that Josh was a better catcher than the Yankee legend, Bill Dickey. And Walter Johnson, the great Senator pitcher, provided his now-famous quote: "There is a catcher that any big league club would like to buy for $200,000. His name is Gibson . . . he can do everything. He hits the ball a mile. And he catches so easy he might as well be in a rocking chair. Throws like a rifle. Bill Dickey isn't as good a catcher. Too bad this Gibson is a colored fellow."

But no big league club was bold enough to grab Josh. It was reported that Pittsburgh Pirate owner William Benswanger had finally decided to sign Gibson and Buck Leonard and was about to offer them a tryout. It never came about. Benswanger said he was talked out of it by Cum Posey, who argued that the signing of Gibson and Leonard would make way for the collapse of the Negro leagues. Others charged that the traditional timidity on the part of white owners had set in, and Benswanger had changed his mind.

Whatever the case, Josh went to work for yet another season with the Grays, this time at a salary of approximately $450 a month. He now had an understudy by the name of Euthumn "Eudie" Napier, a promising receiver who had also grown up on Pittsburgh's North Side and played his sandlot ball there. Yet as long as Josh was healthy, Napier played in his shadow.

When the Grays came to town, it was Gibson and Leonard that the folks came out to see, and, with few exceptions, the pair satisfied their fans.

In June 1939, Josh was hit with an injury, one of the few in his career. Instead of the catcher's usual curse of split fingers or smashed knuckles, Josh came up with a "strawberry." It was a painful burn on his right side, just under the armpit, caused by sliding. All base runners got them from time to time, but Josh's became infected and caused the formation of a carbuncle. Minor surgery was needed to clean and excise the infection, and Josh sat out the schedule for ten days.

During that layoff, he took the time to watch his brother, Jerry, pitch for a Pittsburgh sandlot team. Only twenty-three, and a tall, rangy right-hander, Jerry had little of the natural talent of his brother and was pitching at the time for the Coraopolis Grays, a semipro team from an eastern section of Pittsburgh. Although Jerry managed to pitch one year for the Cincinnati Tigers in the Negro American League, he went through most of his baseball career being known as "the brother of Josh Gibson." Yet on June 17, 1938, with his big brother in attendance, Jerry pitched a no-hitter for the Coraopolis team, and in a rare moment in his life, managed to earn his own headline.

It was a momentary switch, for Josh returned to the Grays' lineup and began clubbing home runs which brought along the ink and the adoration of the sportswriters. One clout—a 465-foot drive in Forbes Field—would be remembered with his longest.

This was a particularly sweet period in Josh's career, for he had to scramble only with the soft-spoken Buck Leonard for the publicity spotlight. Satchel Paige had forsaken Pittsburgh fans in 1938 for the Mexican leagues, and in 1939, after a momentary loss of his pitching arm, he signed on with the Kansas City Monarchs. It meant that the Northeast—Pittsburgh, Philadelphia, and the heart of the upper Midwestern black baseball area—was Josh's territory as far as sportswriters were concerned. And Gibson basked in the attention, played his best baseball, and, by midseason, far outpolled any other catcher in the East-West All-Star game balloting.

He went hitless in that game, however, and the East lost to the West, 4-2. But he would make up for that lapse, as usual, this time in a second East-West game played in September at Yankee Stadium. The game was full of pressure for Josh, not because of the competition, but because prior to it, a white New York newspaperman had given him a buildup the like of which few black players had ever received.

Jimmy Powers, a sportswriter for the New York *Daily News*, wrote a fierce column in which he castigated organized baseball for ignoring the talent of Gibson. "This man would be worth $25,000 a year to any club in baseball," Powers wrote. He went on to say that during the 1939 Gray season Josh had played 103 games and hit 63 homers. In 1936, Powers added, he had hit 84 homers in 130 games. Both figures were undoubtedly fed Powers by Cum Posey or other officials of the Negro leagues, and even if their accuracy could be questioned, Josh's overwhelming power with a bat could not.

Because of Powers's write-up, Josh was scrutinized by white and black fans alike, all interested in seeing if he was really that good. The first two times up, he smashed long, towering drives, but both were caught at the fence. In two more at bats, he was walked intentionally. But finally, in his fifth attempt, he walked to the plate with the bases loaded and crashed a triple to the wall in right field, scoring all three runners and helping the East to a 10-2 win. Those who saw it immediately realized that Jimmy Powers hadn't made up a thing.

The threat to Negro baseball from foreign teams didn't slacken in the winter of 1939-40. An increasing number of black stars played on teams in Latin America, and some were impressed enough with the money and conditions to stay. Most were established, reliable ballplayers such as Cool Papa Bell, and when conscientious players like Bell stayed in Mexico—not just fickle jumpers like Paige—league owners and players alike knew the foreign attraction was bona fide.

Josh first went to Cuba in October of that year and played with a team called the Negro National League Stars. Comprising Josh, Gray pitcher Roy Partlow, Vic Harris, Buck Leonard, Willie Wells, and others, the team played six games against the Cuban Stars in a Havana stadium. By December, Josh was in Puerto Rico with the Santurce club, one of eight teams in the league.

Back in Pittsburgh, Posey made arrangements to expand the Grays' home base to Washington, D.C. That meant that the team would be known as the Washington-Homestead Grays, and it would divide its times between playing home games in Forbes Field in Pittsburgh and in Griffith Stadium on Sundays when the Senators weren't in town. Posey's expansion plans, however, did not make as much off-season baseball news as the increasing parade of jumpers. Sam Bankhead, Josh's close friend and roommate, decided in mid-March to remain with his team in Mexico. Posey quickly reported that he did not expect Josh to follow Bankhead, and promised fans that his catcher would report to the Grays after the close of the Puerto Rican leagues.

In April, the worst fears of Gray fans were confirmed. Instead of Mexico or Puerto Rico, a team from Venezuela offered Josh a contract too lucrative to turn down. It came to $700 a month, with a $1,000 bonus, including travel and living expenses. It was far better than any money he could have made in the States, and he accepted it. He wasn't to be seen on a diamond in Pittsburgh or any other American city for the rest of the year.

The Grays continued to dominate Negro baseball without him. They won the first half of the 1940 season and took a huge trophy back to Homestead. In Venezuela, Josh hit for a .419 average, yet he decided not to stay there, even though the team offered him a three-year contract.

In the winter of 1940-41, Negro league owners wrestled with the problem of whether or not they should permit jumpers back into the league. Cum Posey, with obvious ulterior motives, declared that he was against blackballing the renegades. "Baseball is the only way they know to make a living," he said, and added that it seemed harsh and unwise to prohibit them from playing in the States.

Posey actually knew very well that Gibson wanted to come back and play with the Grays if the money was right, and that left him with the most to gain if jumpers were permitted back into the league. A few weeks later, Posey announced that Josh had been signed to a contract with the Grays which included "the largest salary ever given to a colored player." That meant Josh would just barely earn what he had been getting south of the border.

Posey's optimism and his bullish signing of Gibson was not unfounded, however, for in the two years following the bleak days of 1939, Negro baseball began to prosper along with a national economy which was escaping the Depression. The season of 1941, Posey wrote, looked more financially promising than any in more than a decade, especially if Josh Gibson were to wear a Gray uniform. Such a statement was typical of Posey, a man who compromised principle with financial realities. He was more than willing to welcome star ballplayers back into the fold and forget past grievances if all parties were to benefit. If times looked good for the 1941 season, the presence of Josh—the same man who had jumped his Grays for Venezuela—would make them better. In late February, league owners agreed to drop any ban on jumpers and simply rap knuckles with a $100 fine when they rejoined their American teams.

All seemed right in the Negro baseball world. The Grays headed for Orlando, Florida, to train, and Gibson was reportedly ready to join them.

Again, he didn't. A last-minute offer from a Mexico City club turned his head. Despite the fact that he had signed a contract with Cum Posey, he also signed the Mexican contract. For him, the jump was once again strictly a financial matter. Posey's contract offered him $500 a month for the summer season; the Mexican terms were $800 for each of the next eight months. The offer was better than many major-league contracts. With Gray pitchers Terry McDuffie and Roy Partlow, Josh did not hesitate to return south.

Cum Posey, once again the stern, proud businessman, wasn't about to watch his contract with Gibson become sullied. He immediately instructed his attorneys to file suit against Gibson for "any losses the Grays incur through his leaving." The action carried some weight, for Josh owned a house in Pittsburgh's Hill District and Posey was willing to take possession of it upon a court ruling in his favor. The total amount of damages the Grays were asking was $10,000, principally the deed to Gibson's house.

"Personally, we are the fall guy once more as we were in 1932," Posey wrote in the *Courier*. "In 1932 Gibson signed a contract with the Grays, then used this contract to get more money from the Pittsburgh Crawfords."

Posey's words and actions were headlines in black sports circles, and they gained a lot of support from other owners and fans. Gibson had joined twenty-five top Negro ballplayers in foreign circuits, and that kind of talent loss was telling on the Negro leagues. Chester Washington of the *Courier* wrote that with Josh gone, black baseball had precious few of the really great box-office attractions left.

But Josh wasn't going to be coerced into returning to the Grays. He was making too much money in Mexico and enjoying a standard of living that rivaled major-league conditions in the States. He was playing with Vera Cruz along with Bill Perkins, Willie Wells, Leroy Matlock, and Ray Dandridge. And he played well, hitting long home runs, batting .345, and leading Vera Cruz to the top of the league. In mid-May he received word that a Pittsburgh judge had ruled he had to return to that city in six days or suffer the legal consequences. Josh, perhaps confident that Posey would back down if the issue were pushed, stayed put.

Like virtually all legal actions pressed against recalcitrant Negro ballplayers, Posey's suit had little, if any, effect on Josh. It failed in its primary goal, to get Josh back with the Grays, and Posey, far from being a malicious, vindictive man, had little interest in taking Gibson's home in Pittsburgh from him. During that time, Josh's two children were living with the Masons, the family of Josh's first wife. He had separated from his common-law wife, Hattie. His house in the Hill District affected him and him alone, and if litigation which threatened it wasn't enough to persuade Josh to return to the city, the suit was a failure. Posey knew it and let the prosecution ride until he could think of a better way to get his star attraction back.

Josh, in the meantime, played out the summer season with Vera Cruz and moved on to winter ball in Puerto Rico. He was playing great baseball and hitting with such power that he ran out a home run on the average of every other game. Nothing in his career gave him more pleasure, for in Puerto Rico he was idolized by fans, recognized and surrounded on the streets, and generally regarded as a celebrity wherever he went on the lush, comfortable island.

At the end of the season he had won the batting title and was named most valuable player. Before a noisy San Juan crowd in the Escambron Stadium, he accepted the MVP cup and immense batting trophy. League officials and local politicians showered superlatives upon him as he stood and smiled and warmed to the adoration and praise that was his. Baseball had never been so sweet for him as it was at that moment, and in the face of all the awesome drives he had hit, the games he had won with clutch hits, the pitching duels he had caught, the East-West games he'd starred in before thousands of American fans, the stature he possessed as a star with the Crawfords and the Grays—none of it meant a thing when compared to the honor and gratification he felt in front of a crowd of Spanish fans screaming his name in a strange tongue within a foreign ball park.

The lure of Mexican baseball did not decrease during the years of World War II. Yet the financial prospects of Negro-league teams dramatically improved. Players like Cool Papa Bell, Gibson, and others returned north when American owners could match their Mexican salaries. In February 1942, Josh made known his intention to return to the Grays, and Cum Posey was glad to have him. The $10,000 damage suit was quietly dropped, and Posey returned to his previous practice of being one of Josh's best press boosters.

Even though Josh came back to Pittsburgh weighing a paunchy 230 pounds, Posey knew he was still the best in baseball. And it was a prime time for the game. Wartime rationing and travel limitations made baseball a chief source of entertainment. Crowds of 15,000 to 30,000 regularly came out to Forbes Field and Griffith Stadium to see the Grays. Negro baseball was never richer. Salaries jumped to where Josh was making $1,200 to $1,500 a month. For the first time in his American career, he was making good money for what he did. The game was being generous to him, and in times past that would have meant that Josh's life was good. But exactly the opposite was true. In 1942 he began a desperate slide, a depressed and dark season of the mind and body from which he would not recover.

9

The Slide

He had always possessed a longing for ice cream, great heaps of freshly made vanilla ice cream. As a kid, then as a young man playing with the pros, he ate helping upon helping of it, seemingly immune to putting any weight on his bull-like frame, more than likely replacing the few pounds taken from him with the sweat of a doubleheader. His teammates joked with him as he consumed it, laughing as he laughed, those booming, baritone guffaws that filled hotel lobbies and lounges, clubhouses and buses, for few could help but be infected with the brimming good nature that was Josh.

But with the miles, the games, the aching hours of squatting and traveling and squatting again, the ice cream gave way to beer. He drank it as much as everyone else did, after a game, over cards, in the Crawford Grille or in taverns on the road. Seldom did alcohol go any farther than that. Negro ballplayers took their game very seriously. Drunkenness was not tolerated and seldom seen in the ball park. Beer was a beverage, not a habit or a curse, for Josh and all of his Crawford or Gray teammates in their playing days.

Things changed first in Puerto Rico, then most noticeably in Mexico. Schedules weren't so rigorous, travel was limited, and players found during the winter seasons that they had a lot of leisure time. They played endless card games, pinochle and stud poker, and lounged in hotel lobbies and saloons. In Mexico, when Josh played there in the late 1930s and then in the war

125

years, many of the teams were owned by Mexican liquor magnates, and it was not uncommon for a team owner to reward a clutch hit or a home run with a case of beer. It was gladly accepted in the midst of stifling heat, no air conditioning, and the long hours between games.

Josh began his heavy beer drinking with Sammy Bankhead. The two of them would take cases of rich Mexican beer and see how much of it they could down. They lined up the empty bottles, stacked them in pyramids, and counted them not by twos and threes, but by the dozens. Sammy's wife, Helen, used to watch them with absolute awe, so put off by their capacities that she became a teetotaler. But her abstinence never deterred Sammy and Josh. They occasionally drank between games of doubleheaders, the beer running down their chins as they guzzled it, mixing with the blanket of sweat that poured from them in the Mexican heat. More often, they carried their beer derbies long into the night, sometimes sitting across from each other at a card table with fresh cases at their feet, drinking themselves into oblivion. Yet the next morning the two of them awoke as if they'd been eating ice cream instead of gulping beer, and went about the day, be it a game day or otherwise, without sickness or a trace of a hangover. That, too, amazed Helen Bankhead, and she shook her head and cleaned up the empties.

Just as Helen Bankhead viewed the binges from a distance, so most wives lingered in the background of their husbands' lives. They occasionally traveled with their husbands, but such trips came rarely. Most spouses were unable to penetrate the itinerant life of Negro baseball, a game that ingrained transience into the character of players like Josh and the others. As husbands and fathers, they never really became accustomed to a routine or a stable home life. They kept a clock attuned only to game dates and starting times, and worked everything else—eating, sleeping, laundry, errands, sex—somewhere in between.

During most of his career, Josh traveled alone. After the death of his first wife and the placement of his twin children in the home of his mother-in-law, he concentrated mostly on the responsibilities of a bachelor. In the mid-1930s, he was living with the tall, graceful Hattie, and just as she took a limited interest in his ballplaying in Pittsburgh, she traveled with him only rarely. Once, in 1936, she went to Puerto Rico, where she and Satchel Paige's diminutive wife, Janet, were the only women on the trip.

Her relationship with Josh was soon strained, and his team-mates seldom saw her or heard Josh speak of her. On the few occasions that they did meet her, they were struck with the manner in which Josh would attempt to suppress the high times. He cautioned against cracking jokes around her or getting out of line, adding that Hattie did not like such conduct and didn't tolerate good-natured kidding at all. She exerted a maternal influence on him, it seemed, and his teammates found it baffling that a guy who loved to kid and play practical jokes, to laugh raucously about almost anything as Josh did, would change so around Hattie. They were not surprised to learn of the couple's estrangement by the beginning of the 1940s.

By then the Grays were in Washington on weekends, playing to big crowds at Griffith Stadium. It was there that Josh met Grace, a tiny, disarmingly attractive woman who lived in the capital. She was one of many women who came to Griffith Stadium, especially during the war years when husbands and boyfriends were overseas. Grace's husband was in the service, a fact which made her relationship with Josh possible. She told Josh she was deathly afraid of her spouse, that he was a violent, ruthless man involved in the city's deadly gambling rackets. She insisted Josh share her concerns, for her husband's wrath would spare no one. Her plea didn't impress Josh, for he didn't fear anyone. Instead, he became enamored of the small, chain-smoking beauty, and spent most of his free time with her.

The affair did nothing to enhance Josh's relationship with Hattie, especially when he chose to entertain Grace in Pitts-burgh. Most of Josh's teammates preferred not to get involved in his personal life, and hence few knew much about Grace. But the players' wives knew, and they shared with each other the problems Hattie was going through: the arguments, the scenes. They also knew that the once-domineering Hattie had become virtually unable to control her husband, a man who bucked Negro baseball's most powerful owners with impunity, and who lately did what he pleased.

Grace gradually made more and more public appearances with Josh, sometimes going out with him and Gray teammates for drinks after a game. Her presence at games in Washington or on the road when she traveled with the club became unexceptional. Yet only Sammy Bankhead knew much about the relationship. As the months passed, he realized he was losing his drinking mate, for Josh confided in Sammy that he "was crazy about Grace." Sammy knew there wasn't much he could do even if he wanted to, and he commented to his wife, Helen, that Josh "was a lost cause."

As on his other vices, Grace had little effect on Josh's ballplaying. He anchored the Gray lineup, and with Buck Leonard led the team to championships. His reputation endured. In mid-1942, Mexican team owners traveled all the way to Pittsburgh to try to lure him back south. They showed up outside Forbes Field and began throwing figures at Josh and Bankhead. Their presence so enraged the Poseys that Seward and Cum waived polite protests in favor of an all-out fistfight with the Mexicans. It is not known who won the fight, but the Poseys kept their ballplayers, and the Grays remained the best around.

Though he was only in his early thirties, Josh began at this time to fade physically. He was continually plagued with dizziness and disorientation when he went after high foul flies. Buck Leonard made determined efforts to catch them for him when he could. Josh's batting eye and his power, however, remained unsurpassed, and his throwing arm intimidated the league's boldest base runners. Yet he continued to carry about ten to twenty pounds more than usual, sometimes weighing as much as 230. His knees began to bother him regularly due to cartilage and ligaments stretched from years of squatting behind the plate. He lost his speed, and where he was once a top base stealer, he no longer even took much of a lead off first. In games that were not close, he was replaced by substitute base runners.

In August, although the Grays again won the Negro National League with a record of 26-11, Josh became noticeably fatigued. He complained of feeling poorly and showed signs of stress. He became agitated and nervous, occasionally acting strangely and speaking incoherently. His lapses prompted Vic Harris, the tough Gray field manager, to bench him. Once, when he did, Harris discovered Josh was sitting in the team's bullpen drinking beer, a gross violation of Gray rules. Harris found Josh's behavior doubly troubling because it was something totally out of keeping with Josh's attitude and his way of playing the game. Added to Josh's sometimes erratic behavior, Harris felt it important to keep Gibson out of many games simply to keep him from hurting himself. It was an awkward yet necessary move, yet in all his years of playing with and against Josh Gibson, Harris never thought he would see the day that he would have to protect the awesome catcher from himself.

When the Grays met the Kansas City Monarchs in the 1942 Negro League World Series, Josh was ineffectual. He hit less than .200, and the Grays lost four straight games to the Monarchs. (One game was won by the Grays but protested successfully by the Monarchs because of the appearance of three new players on the Gray roster.)

After the season, doctors told Josh to take a long rest and play no baseball at all, something Josh was reluctant to do. He worried about his poor hitting and played in postseason games in an attempt to regain his old form. The strain brought persistent, painful headaches. Still, Josh refused to slow down. He believed he was too strong, too healthy to remain out of action. He continued to drink and live the high life of the off season.

That lasted until New Year's Day, 1943. He lost consciousness that morning and went into a coma. He was admitted to Pittsburgh's St. Francis Hospital and came out of the coma after several hours. He improved rapidly and was released ten days later. Doctors reported that he had suffered a nervous breakdown, and no further details were ever made public. Cum Posey wrote on January 23 that Josh had simply exhausted himself.

"He [Josh] was worried about his batting and overworked himself in an effort to hit his usual playing stride. He was ordered to take a long rest by his physician at the close of the season, but did not follow the doctor's orders until he was completely run down. He is now the same Josh who never knew the candle had two ends," Posey wrote.

Yet it was more serious than that, even if few people admitted it. Josh's sister, Annie, said that Josh came home from St. Francis with the news that doctors there had told him he had a brain tumor. They reportedly wanted to operate. Josh resisted, Annie said later, "because he figured that if they operated, he'd be like a vegetable."

He never mentioned the diagnosis to anyone else, however, not even Sammy Bankhead. Josh's physician, Dr. E. S. Simms, whose specialty was patient diagnosis, recorded nothing of a tumor in his records. On the few occasions he did examine Josh, he found him to be healthy and robust, if somewhat exhausted from the rigors of his profession. Apart from sporadic lapses or nervous outbursts, Josh was able to bounce back and resume his routine and his relationships with friends as if nothing were amiss. No mention of his problems was made in the months that followed, not even in a lengthy *Courier* interview in which he talked about his career and his greatest thrills as a player.

Cum Posey, however, became concerned over Josh's well-being. He was uncertain of what might happen to Josh if he left Pittsburgh and got out of touch with those who knew him and his problems. Posey revealed that he didn't want Josh to go south for winter baseball. Josh had on occasion lost control there, usually on a drinking binge, and Posey was afraid that foreign officials might make things difficult for the troubled catcher. Josh, on the other hand, refused to miss winter ball. He had always relished the off-season play, and despite his health problems, particularly his bad knees, he made it clear to his friends that he was going to do what he wanted. While he'd always been somewhat disdainful of spring training, saying it was unnecessary after playing a full season of winter ball—"I don't need any practice," he complained to Bankhead, "Not just to play against those little country boys up here," —he had a love for foreign baseball, the one arena which had always been good to him.

In the spring of 1943, he went south with the Grays and their new manager, Candy Jim Taylor, Posey's replacement for Vic Harris, who had gone into the service. The war was beginning to take a heavy toll of both black and white stars of professional baseball. That made Josh an even bigger attraction. He played without any sign of a nervous condition or other problems. He regained his hitting touch and was savage with opposing pitchers. By August he was the East's catcher in the All-Star game and played before 51,000 people at Comiskey Park.

At the season's end, he was hitting an incredible .526 and easily leading the league. He was also again playing himself into the ground. In the World Series with the Birmingham Black Barons, a series which the Grays won in seven games, Josh was exhausted and below par. He did not play well, and Posey realized that it was a necessity to rest him frequently.

Yet the season was another success for Josh as far as the legend of his power was concerned. Fans in Washington, D.C., were awed by his home runs, expecially on one Sunday when Josh hit three in one game, the final blast soaring far into Griffith Stadium's left-field bleachers, a good 460 feet away. As had been the case in Pittsburgh, he was hitting more and longer home runs in a major-league park than any of its resident white sluggers.

Clark Griffith, the owner of the Senators, couldn't help but notice. That year he called Josh and Buck Leonard into his office after a Gray game one Sunday afternoon and talked to them about major-league ball.

"He asked us," Buck Leonard remembered later, " 'Do you fellas want to play major-league ball?' 'Yeah, we wanna play major-league ball.' 'Do you think you could make it?' 'Yeah, we thinks we could make it.' 'So, well, I tell ya,' he says, 'if we started takin' colored into the major leagues, we gonna take your best ones and that's gonna break up your league.' I said, 'Well, if that's gonna be better for the players, then it's all right by me.' But he never did make us an offer, and nothing ever come of it."

Nothing did come of it, for Griffith did not have the courage to be the first to sign black ballplayers. His Senators continued to play well but finished behind the Yankees, and he, like fellow owner Bill Benswanger in Pittsburgh, continued to watch dark-skinned performers in his own ball park who could have helped his cause considerably.

Josh's illness, the headaches and the dizziness, had the most profound effect on his countenance. Gone was that mile-wide smile and his brimming, radiant expression. Instead, he appeared glum, almost sullen, with drooping, lazy eyelids and a look of utter exhaustion. He seemed to have aged almost overnight, gone from a fit, robust athlete in his late twenties to a drawn, haggard hulk appearing as if he were forty or forty-five years old. Still, his moods seldom fit his look. He never complained or let on that he was sick. He seldom lost his raucous, uncontrollable laugh and his urge to tease and torment his friends. He had never been able to sit still very long, or to keep from singing endless tunes and jingles until people told him to shut up, and that didn't stop when the headaches and the seizures came.

Nor did the drinking taper, and with it came unpredictable outbursts. On a number of occasions, in Pittsburgh, and sometimes while traveling with the Grays, Josh would suddenly "lose his wig," as Sammy Bankhead described it. He might carry on like a noisy, recalcitrant drunk, threatening to kill himself, picking fights, or simply making such a commotion that neighbors, bartenders, or hotel managers called the police. Buck Leonard recalled a time in Norfolk, Virginia, when Josh began "acting funny," to such an extent that Cum Posey kept him out of the lineup. That night, while the team was staying in a family-operated rooming house, Josh walked to the toilet in the nude, much to the embarrassment of his teammates and their hosts. He seemed unaware that he was doing anything wrong.

Since Josh never talked to his teammates about what was ailing him, and he was drinking heavily, most of the Grays believed that it was the beer that was making him act strangely. When he didn't drink, they maintained, he was okay. But the frequency of his antics convinced them after a while, that he was surely losing his mind. He was admitted to Washington's St. Elizabeth Hospital, a mental facility, for what the Grays termed "a little boiling out." He returned to the team ten days later, heavily sedated and groggy, and to his teammates, not much improved.

The visits to the sanitarium soon became more and more necessary. They seemed to settle Josh, even though the soothing effects never lasted very long. It was finally determined that Josh should be permitted to play weekend games for the Grays but that he was to be accompanied outside the hospital by two attendants. Josh resented them, as he did almost anyone who treated him as if he were a "sick" person, and on one occasion he ducked away from the pair. The attendants searched all over for him, then contacted Posey and the Grays and spurred them into a flurry of activity in search of their catcher. He was a troubled giant of a man—"not himself," as those around him euphemistically put it—and almost everyone feared the worst. Their worries were for nothing, however, for a few hours later, a teammate came upon Josh inside the Gray team bus. He was sitting in a rear seat, his head against the window, sound asleep.

More than anyone else, Sammy Bankhead realized the extent of Josh's problems, for Bankhead was closest to him at the time and the one person who could control Josh when he began drinking. (One of those who could not was Josh's common-law wife, Hattie. On one occasion when the two were together during that time, Josh ran wildly into the street and so frightened Hattie that she frantically called Vic Harris and his wife for help.) Josh was not a violent person, but he became wild and loud when drunk, and because of his immense bulk, people who did not know him were terrified of him. Even his friends didn't take chances. Josh often charged into the Crawford Grille and demanded five or ten dollars for drinking money. It was promptly given to him. Police called to calm him down or settle a disturbance would not go near him. Once when they did, and managed to shackle him and take him to Pittsburgh's St. Francis Hospital, Josh became so enraged at being strapped inside a straitjacket that with a ferocious burst of strength he ripped the jacket off and walked out of the place.

On other occasions Bankhead was called from his bed in the middle of the night to come and get Josh. Once a caller awakened Sammy and insisted that Josh was about to commit suicide. Bankhead, who always attended to the calls but didn't take Josh's antics as seriously as others did, commented that night to his wife that Josh had again "lost his wig." He found Josh in a hotel, six stories up, standing on a windowsill stark naked, threatening to jump. "Go ahead and jump, then," Sammy said. "See what I care." Then the moment passed, and Josh calmed down and came back to his senses, with his old friend and teammate there to talk and soothe his addled brain.

Bankhead knew well that Josh was still heavily involved with Grace in Washington, and the affair somewhat troubled Sammy. Josh brought Grace everywhere. He insisted during a play-off series with the Birmingham Black Barons that Grace be given transportation by the club to Alabama. If she didn't go, he wouldn't, he told Posey, and Cum arranged her train fare and kept his catcher. Josh also began dressing like her, and the two of them were spectacles to the players and their wives as they went about in matching trench coats and navy pinstriped suits.

If Josh at any time in his life became moody or contrary (apart from the clutches of his illnesses), it was during this period. To his friends, he got that way because of Grace, his awareness of his deteriorating health, and, to some extent, the realization that he wasn't going to be able to play ball much longer. Still, he came out of his depressions almost as soon as they came on. He continued to be a big drink buyer in taverns, the center of parties and get-togethers, the laugher, the carouser.

It was a surprise to some to see him cater to Grace to the extent he did. He went with her everywhere as if to protect her. During ball games he accompanied her to the ladies' room and then stood outside and waited for her. Grace had begun to become a curiosity to the wives of the Grays, for not only did she smoke constantly but she sat alone in the stands and shivered, clutching herself and her wrap, huddling up so that her knees nearly touched her chin. Helen Bankhead had no idea of what was wrong with her, and when she asked her husband, Sammy said Grace had "the drinker's shakes."

It was only a few years later that Sammy revealed that Grace had been taking narcotics of some kind. Her symptoms were consistent with those that Helen Bankhead would see in addicts on the streets thirty years later, but at the time, they were a mystery to her. Sammy didn't go into details, but he was certain of what was happening, and added in an ominous tone that "what she was taking, Josh was taking."

To Bankhead, Josh was still a country boy, a naive, good-natured kid who had been around but still didn't know what trouble he could get into in the big city. Grace was one of those troubles, Sammy insisted, and Josh was unable to resist the temptations she brought his way. Sammy himself had been around, had his share of problems with the bottle and the uncertainties of the game he played, and he knew all too well what was happening to his closest companion. To Helen he described Josh as "a hopeless case" and left the implications of the statement to linger somewhere within their common knowledge of the small woman from Washington. Yet Sammy knew in his soul that it was worse for Josh than that.

Josh himself had no idea of the demons that possessed him, of the voices he heard, and how he could be so strong, so self-sufficient, yet at times so totally unable to control himself. He could feel the physical fire, the pain that tore at his knees, that gave him headaches so wrenching that he couldn't see straight, but that pain was nothing compared to the shadows, the echoes, the forms he thought he saw.

In Washington, D.C., one day, as the team rested between games at Carver Hall, a government-supported rooming house, a few Gray players became aware of strange sounds coming from Josh's second-floor room. When they got closer, a few of them gathering on the grass below the window, they realized that Josh was sitting alone by the window, staring vacantly, engaged in a conversation with someone only he could see.

"C'mon, Joe, talk to me," he said, "why don't you talk to me?"

For long moments, his teammates were dumbfounded, wondering who and what Josh was talking to, not daring to interrupt. Finally it became clear to them as Josh mumbled on, still gazing into space.

"Hey, Joe DiMaggio, it's me, you know me. Why don't you answer me? Huh, Joe? Huh? Why not?"

And as his teammates silently watched, he droned on and on.

"C'mon, Joe, you know me. You ain' gonna answer me?"

10

An Athlete Dying Young

In 1944, Josh's playing status became threatened by the military draft. An earlier exemption for physical reasons—his bad knees, his nervous problems, headaches—was reviewed, and his Pittsburgh draft board requested him to come in for a new exam. The board had reclassified Bankhead, and had drafted Howard Easterling, another close friend and teammate, and Josh feared he was next. But army doctors were as dubious about his health as his regular physicians had been, and Josh was given permanent 4F status. The Grays' Buck Leonard, who had his share of knee problems, was also exempted, a development which did not displease Cum Posey.

In late February 1944, Josh went to Hot Springs, Arkansas, to get into shape to play. He had not played winter ball, and he was again overweight. Bankhead, who had been told by the army that he would not be called up until June, went with him. Cum Posey, meanwhile, went about looking for a backup catcher. As his brother, See, stated, Josh wasn't effective in the 1943 series against Birmingham "because he was burned out by the time the Series started."

Posey wasn't the only owner looking for additional talent. Since the beginning of World War II, rosters of black and white teams alike had been thinned by the armed forces. Though the war was the chief concern in the country, the national push for racial equality and equal opportunity which had been given impetus years before with the Roosevelt administration was now

137

stronger than ever. Baseball was a trivial but glaring example of racial discrimination, especially with the depletion of major-league talent due to the draft. There seemed no better time to end the hypocrisy of the color ban, and blacks and whites alike—owners, players, journalists, politicians—battered away at the issue.

In early 1942, Jackie Robinson and Nate Moreland, then both young Negro league standouts, had shown up at the training camp of the Chicago White Sox at Pasadena, California's Brookside Park, and requested a chance to try out for the team. Robinson was wearing his UCLA varsity jacket. But both men were refused by White Sox manager Jimmy Dykes. Dykes said Robinson was worth $50,000 to any team he signed with, but he personally couldn't sign black players unless he had permission from league owners.

That fraternity, the same men who had sustained the unofficial color ban for a half century, was beginning to show signs of weakening. Owners like Clark Griffith had said as far back as 1938 that the time was "not far off" when blacks would be signed to major-league contracts. In the early 1940s they were saying it again. Names of players like Paige, Bell, Gibson, Monte Irvin, Jackie Robinson, and many others were mentioned over and over again as surefire prospects. Big-league managers like Leo Durocher, Gabby Hartnett, and Bill McKechnie insisted that they would welcome black players, and white major leaguers, as they had for years, maintained they would welcome black teammates. Powerful white sportswriters such as Jimmy Powers, Shirley Povich, and Heywood Broun railed against the injustice.

All those outraged white voices, however, were part of an old refrain as far as Josh and other black stars were concerned. They had heard it before, as far back as the early 1930s, and they were not so naive now as to get their hopes up. As Buck Leonard said, "We didn't think nothin' of it."

Josh, likewise, seldom concerned himself with the controversy, the rumors of tryouts, or the frustration of it all. In the mid-1940s he was almost totally occupied with his own problems, his fading health, his nerves and his mental instability, his affair with Grace. He had long ago resigned himself to the realities of his color, and he wasn't waiting for something like destiny to tap him on the catcher's mask. Just getting in shape for the coming Gray seasons, ones in which he was making good money and playing before impressive crowds, was work enough.

In his last three seasons with the Grays—1944, 1945, and 1946—Josh became something that he had never been known for: a singles hitter. He was only in his early thirties, but his bad knees, his nervous problems, and his excessive drinking served to make him a negligible home-run threat at a time in his career in which he should have been hitting a lot of homers. Babe Ruth, by comparison, hit his record-breaking total of 60 homers for the Yankees in 1927 when he was thirty-two. He followed that year with home run totals of 54, 46, 49, 46, 41, and 34, tapering finally in 1934 when he was thirty-nine years old. Henry Aaron, likewise, hit 44 homers in 1966 when he was thirty-two, and followed that with seven seasons of 20 or more, culminating with a career high of 47 in 1971 when he was thirty-seven.

Josh, however, was not hitting them as far or as often as he had earlier. In 1944, at the age of thirty-three, he hit only 6 homers in 39 NNL games with the Grays. The next year, he hit 8 in 44 games, for two-year total of 14. Still, his batting average remained high, mainly because he still had his steady, unflinching eye and a bat control which made him a difficult out. While he was hitting only 8 homers in 1945, he was leading the league with a .393 batting average. There wasn't a receiver in Negro baseball of whom people thought more highly.

Negro baseball continued to thrive during the last two years of the war. Salaries continued to soar, especially for stars. Satchel Paige was reported to be making as much as $7,000 a month. Steady performers such as Josh and Buck Leonard were up to the $1,500 mark. Still, league officials worried about what might happen at the war's end when Office of Price Administration restrictions on travel and rationed goods would be lifted. If people went on picnics instead of to the ball park, they wondered, would Negro baseball flounder as it had through most of the 1930s?

Their concerns, however, were overshadowed by yet another development in baseball. After years of promises, Jackie Robinson of the Kansas City Monarchs was finally signed by Branch Rickey and the Brooklyn Dodgers in October 1945. At twenty-six, Robinson prepared to report to the Montreal Royals in the Dodger farm system for the 1946 season. All of baseball, particularly players and fans of the black leagues, anticipated his debut with more intensity than the game had ever known. Johnny Wright, a Gray right-handed pitcher, was signed a few months later and joined Robinson in Montreal. Rickey also signed Baltimore Elite catcher Roy Campanella and pitcher Don Newcombe of the Newark Eagles. But both Campanella and Newcombe were assigned to a lower-level minor-league team in Nashua, New Hampshire, and few expected either of them to progress as fast as Robinson or Wright.

The fortunes of the newly signed black players. specifically Robinson's, dominated sports news in black papers. His four hits on opening day in Montreal, including a home run, made headlines. The fact that he and the other black minor leaguers were playing for less money than they would have been making in the Negro leagues—Robinson was paid $400 a month for Montreal and would have been offered $600 for the Monarchs; Wright got the same and would have made $650 with the Grays; Campanella and Newcombe were each making $175 to $200 less than in black league play—was gladly overlooked.

Instead, white club owners like Rickey and the Giants' Horace Stoneham were pressed by sportswriters concerning other black players they intended to sign. The list was impressive, for Stoneham and Rickey had done their homework and knew black talent intimately. They had their eye on Newark's Larry Doby, Monte Irvin, and Leon Day; Philadelphia's Bus Clarkson; Baltimore's Sammy Hughes. Other strong black candidates for white-league contracts were Roy Welmaker and Jerry Benjamin of the Grays, Sammy Jethroe of Cleveland; Bill Ricks, Frank Austin, Tommy Butts, Henry Kimbro, Tommy Sampson, Piper Davis, and Verdel Mathis. The names went on and on, as long as the Negro leagues were deep in black talent.

But Josh wasn't on the list. Nor were Satchel Paige, Buck Leonard, Cool Papa Bell, and a number of other league fixtures. All were considered too old to make the grind of minor leagues, to go through the acclimatizing process that white owners believed black players and white fans needed before a Jackie Robinson was inked into a major-league scorecard. The possibility of taking any one of them and simply putting him right into a major-league lineup was not considered. Baseball had taken its time in signing a black, and it would not be hurried now that the initial step had been taken.

The fact that Josh had won the Negro National League batting title with a .393 average in 1945 meant little. He was thirty-three and in poor health. He was slow, his knees were aching continually, and the stories of his excessive drinking abounded. He had, for example, missed the 1945 East-West All-Star game because Cum Posey had benched him for "breaking training rules," meaning that he had again gone on a drinking binge. He had also played badly for much of the 1945 season, and young Roy Campanella of Baltimore was a better choice for the East All-Star squad. In the last part of the season, however, Josh redeemed himself with a remarkable hitting spree. He led the Grays to consecutive victories over contending clubs and helped them win their sixth straight NNL title. Even though he soured and went two for fifteen in the World Series against Cleveland (the Grays lost it in four straight), he was picked as the top Negro-league catcher for the year.

That winter he went south to play for Santurce in Puerto

Rico. There he learned of Robinson's signing with the Dodgers, and though it is difficult to establish a relationship between the two events, Josh again fell prey to fits of erratic behavior. Late in the winter season he was found wandering nude in San Juan. When police took him into custody, he told them he was trying to get to the airport. He was committed to a sanitarium, and shortly, as he had always done before, he showed signs of improvement. He was released and allowed to leave the country.

One person who would have looked with relish on the fortunes of Jackie Robinson in 1946 never got the chance. On March 28, Cum Posey died at the age of fifty-five. It is uncertain just how gratified Posey would have been at Robinson's breakthrough, but the powerful and articulate baseball magnate would have had a lot to say about it.

With his death, the Grays were deprived of their lifeblood. Even though Posey's brother, Seward, carried on with the team, the Grays were never again to benefit from the sure and guiding baseball hand that was Cum's. As long as he was alive, the team went about its schedule with steady confidence, even when it wasn't stocked with the best talent, for Posey's shrewd and dominating sense of organization settled for nothing less.

Following Cum's death, the Grays, for the first time in years, played lackluster baseball. They no longer intimidated the league, finished third behind Newark and Philadelphia in the first half with an 18-15 record, then floundered in the second half with a 9-13 slate. Without Cum Posey sitting in the stands, picking his teeth, eating his favorite candy (marshmallow "tobies"), giving signs to his field manager, studying the strengths and weaknesses of his ball club and gauging ways to make it stronger, the Grays were not the team they had always been.

Part of the decline was also due to Josh, for 1946 was another difficult year for him. As the season wore on, his knees began to bother him severely. By August he was out of the lineup for weeks at a time. Both knees were so battered he could hardly move around. Still, he was voted to both East-West games. In the first he batted only twice, singling the second time up, then being lifted for a pinch runner. It was only the fourth inning, and the 16,000 people in Griffith Stadium were very aware of the fact that the overweight, haggard player who limped off the field that day was but a shell of the Josh Gibson they had once known.

In Chicago's Comiskey Park at the second East-West game of 1946, Josh never hit the ball out of the infield in three tries. There were 45,000 fans in the stands that day, and none of them realized that it would be the last time they would ever see Josh Gibson play baseball.

There was no way Jimmie Crutchfield could have known it, but with the same foresight that had moved him to begin his personal scrapbook fifteen years earlier, he went to the East dugout that day in Chicago to look up Josh. Crutch had spent a night with him in 1945 after a Gray-Chicago American Giant game. The two of them talked baseball and remembered the times, the golden years of the Crawfords and Gus Greenlee, and a lot of things that had happened since them. As they reminisced, the extent of Josh's drinking became very apparent to Crutchfield. Whereas Josh had always drunk beer, that night in Chicago he was drinking straight whiskey—shot after shot of it, without a chaser. When he stopped in the dugout the following year, Crutch yelled at Gibson, "Hey, Josh. I want your autograph." It was a flattering yet self-conscious moment for Gibson, and he replied, "Hey, Crutch, I should be getting *your* autograph." Nevertheless, he signed a piece of paper Jimmie had brought along. Crutchfield took it home and put it with his scrapbook, then later transferred it to a safe-deposit box.

It was small, gratifying moments like those that made up most of Josh's victories that year. The sports pages were dominated by the feats of Jackie Robinson. Few players in the history of the sport have had their every game so closely monitored as Robinson did that year. If it wasn't Robinson, it was Campanella,

Wright, Newcombe, and Roy Partlow—each man seeing his every play in the minor leagues carefully scrutinized. With each success, each four-for-four day, especially by Robinson, black baseball fans were certain that at any minute one of the most aggravating obstacles in sports equality would be shattered.

If Josh had any hope for the future, it lay not with himself but with another Gibson who was playing good ball in Pittsburgh. That summer he sat in the stands and watched Josh, Jr., play sandlot baseball for the Pittsburgh Stars. Only sixteen, five feet, ten inches tall, Josh, Jr., was a quick, agile second baseman with the same eye for hitting that his father had.

The boy, however, had never had a close relationship with his father. Josh occasionally brought Josh, Jr., along to Gray games and let him be team batboy, but he didn't spend much time with him. The twins had been raised by their grandmother and aunts, and they harbored ill feelings for a father who had had so little time for his children.

He also, at times, supported them badly. Gray teammates tried not to notice when Josh's mother-in-law, and occasionally his own kids, showed up at the ball park to beg money from him. As big a star as Josh Gibson was, his son and daughter grew up in poverty, often engendering the pity of schoolmates who saw how quiet and withdrawn the twins were and how impoverished.

On many nights Josh slept in the same bed as his boy, yet Josh, Jr., actually had a closer relationship with Sammy Bankhead than with his father. Bankhead chided Josh about it and attempted to convince him that he had to pay more attention to his family, but it was very nearly impossible for Sammy to alter a routine that Josh had known most of his life.

By the end of the 1946 season, Josh was hardly playing at all. Satchel Paige put together a touring all-star team for postseason exhibitions against major-league all-star teams, and perhaps due to his long-standing competition with Josh, Satchel didn't sign him to the team. More likely, Josh wasn't able to play.

In the fall of the year, his drinking and his moodiness increased. He hung out at the Crawford Grille and other haunts in Pittsburgh's Hill District and on the North Side. His knees were bothering him so much that he didn't go south to play for the winter. Without the game, without the enforced routine that dictated what he did every day, Josh was lost. Ted Page saw him occasionally, noticed that Josh was losing weight and looking more drawn than ever, and Page invited him to his bowling alley. He later persuaded Josh to work out at the YMCA on Center Avenue, and Josh even joined a volleyball league there. But most often he spent long hours on a bar stool. Page came across him one night in a tavern and saw Josh clutching the collar of a stranger and violently shaking him. Seeing Page, Josh bellowed, "Tell this man who hit the longest ball anyplace! Tell him!"

By this time, Josh was no longer seeing Grace. Their relationship had been broken off at the end of the war at her request. She told Josh she was afraid her husband would kill her if he knew of their affair, and though Josh was reluctant to break off, she insisted. He did not take up with anyone new and maintained a haphazard relationship with Hattie.

That December, he turned thirty-five, a young man by most standards except the one that counted most to him: his playing age. He was an old catcher with ravaged knees, and he began to reveal it in his disposition. He was living in his mother's house at 2410 Strauss on the North Side, drinking heavily, complaining of headaches, dizziness, and his knees. Yet there were days when he was able to rebound and go about as cheerful and gregarious as he had always been. His closest friends and teammates were generally unaware of how sick he was, for he seldom complained to them about anything. Even to the family physician, Dr. Earl Simms, he mentioned no particular ailments, and Simms considered him in good, albeit run-down health.

Josh, however, was suffering from chronic hypertension, a

condition which went largely untreated at the time. He fell into depressions and continued to drink excessively. By the New Year, 1947, he had dropped from a playing weight of 220 pounds, and on a frame that was muscular and solid, to a hollow 180.

The loss of weight was a key to Josh's emotional state, for he had always considered himself a bull of a man. He had been prized for his strength, his endurance, his awesome power. Now that was dwindling away, and he knew it every time he saw his reflection in the mirror behind the long bar in the Crawford Grille. It was that realization that was killing him, and not, as so many have speculated, the prospect of Jackie Robinson's being the first black man to wear a major-league uniform. Josh, like so many of his teammates who had missed out on a chance to make the majors primarily because of age, was not one to brood over it or feel that he had been slighted, or cheated, or victimized. More frustrating to him was the specter of being a has-been, of no longer being able to play baseball, of feeling his life's obsession drift away from him with every spasm of dizziness and every shot of pain from his knees.

He was also stung by the fact that he would no longer be able to make a handsome living playing ball. He was the same Josh who had signed two contracts in two days in 1932, then played the value of one against the other. He was the same Josh who had held out in 1937 against Gus Greenlee, then jumped to the Dominican Republic; and the same man who played through the risk of two years of obscurity in South America for the salary alone. As energetic as he had been, as strong, as motivated, and, most pointedly in 1947, as young as he was, the thought of no longer being able to command top dollar to smash a baseball for somebody was devastating.

His health grew worse in the first weeks of January. He drank excessively and made no effort to stay in shape. He developed an acute case of bronchitis from the Pittsburgh winter. Still, he went about from day to day. Ted Page saw him on the corner of Center and Kilpatrick, Saturday night, January 18, and the two of them exchanged small talk. Ted saw that Josh had been drinking, that he appeared tired and thin, but he had no reason to believe that Josh was extremely sick.

Later that night, Josh was in the Crawford Grille. He complained of an intense headache. He was taking medication, believed to be some form of sedative, but said it didn't help much. The next day, Sunday the nineteenth, he again complained of a headache, this time saying it was so severe that he thought he might need a doctor.

The story of the final hours of his life has many versions. Josh's sister, Annie Mahaffey, tells a most remarkable one. To Robert Peterson in *Only the Ball Was White,* she said that Josh came home the night of the nineteenth and told his mother he felt sick. Peterson wrote:

He said that he believed he was going to have a stroke. Mrs. Gibson said, "Shush, Josh, you're not going to have no stroke," but she sent him to bed. The family gathered around his bedside and waited for a doctor while Josh laughed and talked. Then he sent his brother Jerry to the homes of friends to collect his scattered trophies and his radio and bring them home. "So Jerry came back about 10:30," Mrs. Mahaffey said, "and we were all laughing and talking, and then he had a stroke. He just got through laughing and then he raised up in the bed and went to talk, but you couldn't understand what he was saying. Then he lay back down and died right off."

In other stories, and interviews given other writers, Mrs. Mahaffey did not relate such a scene. Dr. Simms remembers being summoned from his office to the Garden Theater, a movie house where, the doctor was told, Josh had suffered a stroke. He was unconscious and remained so as he was taken to his mother's house. There he was given more shots, but he did not respond. Dr. Simms left the house that evening with Josh sleeping deeply. At what Dr. Simms estimated to have been one thirty in the morning of January 20, Josh silently passed away.

The funeral took place in the Macedonia Baptist Church on Bedford Avenue. It was but a few paces away from sandlots where Josh first started hitting a ball. The friends he'd once played with there showed up; some carried his coffin. Hundreds of others attended, making the funeral one of the largest the city of Pittsburgh had ever seen. Yet it was tiny in view of what it could have been, in consideration of the thousands of fans Josh had left across the country and in foreign cities. His death was the headline on the front pages of black newspapers all over the country, papers with readers who had struggled to get pennies together to see him play. Now they grieved at the loss of so brilliant a talent through silent moments over the latest copy of the *Courier,* or the *Defender,* or the *Amsterdam News.* Few could personally pay their respects.

His former teammates—Crawfords such as Crutchfield, Paige, Bell, and Charleston—were scattered about the country, and most missed the funeral. Pallbearers were relatives and a few Gray teammates living in Pittsburgh during the off-season. Gus Greenlee attended with John Clark and other associates. The press, the sportswriters who had lyricized Josh's blasts through the years, showed up in force. The Poseys came up from Homestead, minus the late Cum; other Gray officials came and stood shoulder to shoulder with those from the Black Yankees, the Crawfords, the Elite Giants. Sammy Bankhead had to send his regrets from South America. Winter baseball kept him from witnessing the burial of his closest friend.

Rumors of Josh's emotional and physical problems in his final days flowed through the funeral crowd. Many asked about the circumstances of his death, the stroke that had killed him, yet most shook their heads and reminded themselves that it had only been a few years before that Josh Gibson had been the brawny, shiny-faced kid from the lots who had come up so fast the newspapers couldn't even spell his name right.

He was buried in Pittsburgh's Allegheny Cemetery. He left

his family with little money; nothing for even a gravestone of any kind. No plaque would tell who was buried there or what he had done. A small metal oval with a plot number on it marked the grave; it was furnished by the county.

11

Transition

At Josh's death, the Crawfords had been gone almost a decade. Gus Greenlee had scrambled to keep afloat financially after the team's demise in 1938, overseeing his holdings to the point where he once personally manned the skillets at his Grille. He did manage to maintain his strong political standing in Pittsburgh's North Side even though proud Greenlee Field had been torn down, but his shiny green team buses no longer crisscrossed the country, and his fighters, most notably John Henry Lewis, had failed to bring him many titles. All were reverses that Greenlee the sportsman found difficult to deal with, but which Greenlee the businessman could overcome.

In the mid-1940s, when Negro baseball hit its financial peak, Gus tried to reorganize the Crawfords and get a team back into the league. Other league owners were skeptical, however, especially since they no longer needed Greenlee's financial input. They successfully blocked his efforts. The Crawfords were never to rise again. Their chief publicist, John Clark, who had inundated black papers with Crawford copy during the team's fat years, and who had carried on a long public feud over league matters with Cum Posey, even went to work for his chief nemesis in 1942, and thus began turning out superlatives for once-hated Grays.

In 1947, however, a year which would mark the beginning of the modern era of professional baseball, few people in the game were really paying any attention to the doings of the Negro

150

leagues. It was the year of Jackie Robinson. Period. The Negro leagues continued to exist, and they played competitive schedules, but numbers of their best young players were being signed by big-league clubs. Late in the 1947 season, Larry Doby of the Newark Eagles joined the Cleveland Indians, becoming the first black player in the American League. Others followed, some performing well, some doing only fairly and failing to break out of the minor leagues for long. But with Robinson leading the way, and playing superbly, black ball players appeared finally to have a permanent place in major-league baseball.

The following year, Satchel Paige was signed by Bill Veeck of the Cleveland Indians. Already forty-two, and a shadow of the pitcher he had been for the Crawfords and other Negro league teams, Paige had finally made it. With Josh in his grave, and Bell, Charleston, Leonard, and the other old-time Negro league standouts too old to compete, Satchel was to be the only Crawford to play in two eras. That meant something special to Negro league fans, something different from Robinson's breakthrough. When Satch made his Indian debut in Chicago's Comiskey Park, the same place in which Josh and Mule Suttles and Buck Leonard and Jimmie Crutchfield had delighted black crowds in those exquisite East-West games through the years, the creaking South Side Chicago stadium was packed with black faces. Negro baseball fans in that city refused to pass up the chance to see at least one of the old-time barons finally accept his garland.

Josh, of course, was not there to see it, nor was his family. They carried on anonymously in their spare Pittsburgh homes. Little of his glory or the stature of his career marked their lives. Josh, Jr., was a quiet, withdrawn teen-ager, a thin boy with little of the ebullience and strength of his father. He could play ball, however, and under the close scrutiny of Sammy Bankhead, it looked as if he might have a future in the pros. In 1948, he was the first black player signed into the Mid-Atlantic League and played with the Youngstown Colts. At first he caught, but later moved to second base. The next year, he played with the Grays, and his presence on his father's renowned team was duly noted. (The Grays by that time, however, were losing money, and owner Rufus Jackson was about to fold the team.)

In 1950, Josh, Jr., was signed with a Pittsburgh Pirate farm team in Farnham, Quebec, a member of the Class A Provincial League. His manager there was Sammy Bankhead, the first black manager in minor-league baseball, and Bankhead looked with pride on his young second baseman. Some said Josh, Jr., was too young, that he was being brought up too soon. Yet the boy's determination was fierce. He had an awesome legend to live up to.

Unfortunately, he was by then plagued with hypertension, the same malady which had figured in his father's death. Yet the crushing blow to his big-league ambitions came in that first year when he broke his foot. He never sufficiently recovered from the break or regained the form that had impressed major-league scouts. Soon he was out of organized baseball. The test of his heritage had been short, relatively painless, and now was over.

That same year, Gus Greenlee suffered a stroke and was unable to carry on his business dealings. His condition worsened and he was admitted to the Veterans Administration Hospital in Aspinwall, Pennsylvania. He stayed there for five weeks, then was returned to his home in Pittsburgh, where he needed constant care. In 1951, the Crawford Grille was completely destroyed by fire. It was the final setback for Greenlee, for with the loss of the restaurant, and a pending U.S. government suit for back taxes, Gus's fortune was depleted. Friends said that due to his physical condition, he was never told of the Grille fire. On July 7, 1952, he died in his home.

That same year, Josh's brother, Jerry, contracted three-day pneumonia and died. He was only thirty-three. Though he possessed little of the talent of his brother, Jerry played a lot of baseball and made the pros for a year with the Cincinnati Tigers. Like Josh, Jerry was vigorously supported by his mother, Nancy, a perky, excitable woman who squealed with joy when she watched her sons play ball, and sorrowfully mourned their deaths. She had lost her hasband, Mark, in the early 1940s, before Josh's death, also from pneumonia, but it was the loss of her two sons, once so strong and indestructible, that grieved her until her own death in 1963 at the age of seventy-one.

Nancy Gibson's death left only her daughter, Annie, the family's youngest child. Annie married Elmer Mahaffey and remained on Pittsburgh's North Side. But her life was a private one, and only seldom was she to be known as Josh Gibson's sister.

Josh's son and daughter also entered a period in which they were to lead quiet, private lives, something neither of them minded.

Except among his close friends, the memory of Josh Gibson would become dim and mostly forgotten in the 1950s. Sports fans were eagerly charting the careers of a whole new breed of black professionals, sparkling, aggressive talents, and, most significantly, playing in the glow of the big time. The second half of the century realized a new era in sport, and its fans, both black and white, could be excused for celebrating such progress, even if it meant temporarily blotting out the memory of past stars.

12

Cool Papa

The Crawfords were by no means the greatest Negro baseball team of all time. Rube Foster's Chicago American Giants may have been, or Cum Posey's methodical, masterful Homestead Grays. In certain seasons, New York's Lincoln Giants, with Pop Lloyd and Smokey Joe Williams, or the Kansas City Monarchs, with Satchel Paige, were as flawless as any nine black men on a baseball field had ever been. Yet for some reason it is the Craws, the four-name team—Gus Greenlee's Pittsburgh Crawfords— who bring back the memories, who fire the stories and crackle the skin with all the style and resonance of the times.

They throve during the country's most dismal period—1932 to 1936—years in the teeth of the Depression. And they did so with class. The Crawfords meant black pride years before that phrase became a cliché. They were one of the greatest collections of colorful, distinct, awesome stars in sports history. They were a textbook assembly of what a winning baseball team should be: lean, lightning-quick Cool Papa Bell in center field, flanked by the fierce Jimmie Crutchfield and dependable Ted Page; do-everything third baseman Judy Johnson throwing across the diamond to the hard-hitting, brawling first baseman, perhaps baseball's most skillful all-around player, Oscar Charleston; Josh, the rock behind the plate and total power at bat; Satchel pitching. Other stars complemented them along the way—Bill Perkins, Sam Bankhead, Chester Williams, Leroy Morney, Jake Russell, Harry Kincannon, Sam Streeter, Leroy Matlock,

Rap Dixon. But it was the meat of that starting lineup—Bell, Crutchfield, Page, Johnson, Charleston, Gibson, and Paige— which became so easy to recite, as thousands of little black kids in Pittsburgh once had, and, finally, so difficult to forget.

Even forty years later.

Cool Papa finally went back to St. Louis, the place where it had all started for him some thirty years before. Then, as an eager kid of nineteen, he was about to take full-time work in a packing plant, a steady, secure job for a black in 1922. But so crafty and slick a leadoff hitter and center fielder was he, no packinghouse job could outbid a professional baseball club for his services, and Cool Papa Bell cut grooves in base paths instead of beef shanks. The legend that he became, the headlines and columns and tributes he earned in all those years of Negro baseball—none of it counted for much in 1950 when his legs went and his career was over and he became just another unemployed black man. Instead of working in a packinghouse or an ice shed, he signed on as a night security man in St. Louis's City Hall.

At home, Bell remained married to his most ardent fan, his wife, Clarabelle. She was the same woman who had traveled with him through the years, who had kept his voluminous scrapbooks, and who had gently endured his itinerant life. Now, in his later years, Clarabelle worried about Cool in his job at the Hall, worried that he'd have to use the gun he wore. She also suffered through the uncertainties of her own solitary nights. Yet she made the best of things, as she had done for so long.

During the day, Cool Papa occasionally took in a Cardinals game at Busch Stadium, or he talked the game at the barbershop, or lingered with friends and relatives. He kept his name in the phone book, went to church every Sunday, and tried to keep his health.

Baseball spent most of its time watching the new generation of black players: the marvelous Jackie Robinson, Larry Doby, then the parade of such do-everything talents as Willie Mays, Ernie

Banks, and Latins Roberto Clemente and Orlando Cepeda. The gates were open, and black ballplayers crashed them with a vengeance—especially kids like Campanella, Newcombe, Banks, and Mays, who had played a few seasons with Negro teams. The major leagues throve on their presence. Robinson's base running injected a reckless excitement not seen since the likes of Pepper Martin or Ty Cobb. Willie Mays's 1954 World Series catch—over the head on a dead run with his back to the infield—of Vic Wertz's drive was an unforgettable masterpiece. Recorded on film, it has become ingrained in the memories of generations of baseball fans.

As gratifying as the assertion of black talent was to the game, it excluded any substantial participation by the established stars of the Negro leagues. By some strange coincidence, no legendary player except Satchel Paige had enough good years in him to play in both black and white baseball. Paige was signed when he was already in his forties, and though he still had enough guile to get batters out for a few years, he wasn't the Paige who had set the black leagues aglow for twenty years.

Roy Campanella came close to bridging the gap, establishing himself as a protégé of Biz Mackey with the Baltimore Elite Giants and then breaking in with the Dodgers at age twenty-eight in 1948 and starring for ten years. Monte Irvin, Larry Doby, and Minnie Minoso also played solid years in both leagues. But none of the headline stars of the Negro leagues were able to make the jump, to overcome the fact that they had been born ten years too soon. Gibson, Bell, Charleston, Mule Suttles, Judy Johnson, Martin Dihigo, Buck Leonard—all were simply too old, even by Negro league standards, which allowed many of them to play into their late forties and fifties, to enjoy even a couple of seasons of the big time, of top salaries, first-class playing conditions, and total recognition.

Cool Papa Bell knew it every time he walked over to Busch Stadium and sat unrecognized in the crowd. It didn't bother him, for he had spent his life in the shadows and he wasn't about to complain. A few of the black major leaguers sensitive enough to know who went before them occasionally got in touch with Cool Papa and invited him into the clubhouse after a game. Lou Brock was one. Ernie Banks, whom Bell had scouted and coached as part of the Kansas City Monarch organization, was another. They listened when Cool mentioned some of the things he used to do as a base runner, how he told hitters to stand in the back of the box, putting the catcher a few inches farther away from things and making it easier for him to steal second. They listened while Cool Papa talked; then they caught team buses headed for first-class hotel rooms, and Bell walked back to his apartment on Dickson Street, not far from where Busch Stadium used to be.

The old stadiums told a lot about the game. Named Busch, Forbes, Connie Mack, Crosley, Briggs, they left no doubt as to who owned the team, the field, the baseballs, and who, more importantly, set its standards. The new stadiums may be more democratic—Three Rivers, Riverfront—more spacious and better built, but they have also put the fan farther away from the action and the faces of the players, and they've put synthetic rugs where grass once grew. There is something strange about an infield with no base paths, something revolting about a bloop fly that bounces fifteen feet over the head of an outfielder. When Bill Veeck bought the Chicago White Sox in 1976, he touched a sympathetic streak in baseball fans in that city when he announced that White Sox Park would again be known as Comiskey Park and that he was bringing real grass back to the infield. Past owners had installed synthetic turf only in the infield, a move dictated more by tight finances than divided sensibilities. Veeck then permitted fans to show up one preseason afternoon and take away the nylon turf with their bare hands. They did so, every inch of it, viciously, as if the spongy green chemical they were removing represented a corrupt regime.

By the early spring of 1971, Cool Papa hadn't made it over to the Cardinals' newly built Busch Stadium, but he knew he probably would sooner or later. He did, however, welcome the chance to talk baseball with almost anyone who stopped by. It was his night off from work; it wouldn't be long before he would retire for good. He was sixty-eight years old, and the city and his legs were telling him that he should quit.

Though St. Louis was far from being a hotbed of the black social upheaval of the 1960s, it contained a sizable black population which, as in most Midwestern big cities, had been largely unable to rejuvenate or flee from an aging, deteriorating central city. On a cold February night, I drove through the heart of it, away from downtown and up Easton Avenue toward Bell's apartment. The neighborhoods along the way reflected their problems, with vacant lots, boarded-up storefronts, and garish murals of the martyred Malcolm X.

Dickson Street was just off Easton, and Bell's place just down from an old Sinclair service station. It was a solid, red-brick two-flat, built seventy years ago by contractors who couldn't conceive of such homes ever wearing out. Bell told me to ring once—two rings would be for the Williamses upstairs. Clarabelle Bell peeked through the blinds, then she and Cool Papa showed me into their living room.

Bell was tall—six-foot-two—but fuller-faced than in his playing pictures. His short black hair had no gray and gave him the look of a man ten years younger.

"You sit right down," he said, and directed me to a lime-green sofa against one wall. The room was warm and well-lit, furnished with comfortable furniture and shelves full of knick-knacks, no trophies, but a few mementos of Bell's playing days. It was a sitting room—quiet, comfortable, very much reflecting the established, civilized routine of an elderly couple. A jar of hard candy lay on the glass of a coffee table, and beneath the glass were snapshots of nephews and nieces. The Bells had no children of their own.

Mrs. Bell poured me a soft drink, then went over to the front window.

"Checking on your car," she said. "We got to watch it all the time."

Cool Papa sat down and asked me if I wanted to use the bathroom. Some people, he said, are afraid to ask. Then he picked up a wedge of fresh lemon and bit into it.

"I got to suck this for my voice," he said. "I been talking to much lately."

He had because now, twenty years after he had retired from playing and coaching, he was gradually being rediscovered. Renewed interest in the Negro leagues had bloomed in 1969 when Satchel Paige was inducted into Baseball's Hall of Fame, and his induction, and the publicity given his life and exploits, had once again brought Negro baseball alive, particularly among a generation of baseball fans who had never known a segregated game. The push was aided enormously by publication of Robert Peterson's *Only the Ball Was White*, the first definitive history of the leagues and players. Cool Papa was a prominent inclusion, and the mention that he was still alive and well brought fans old and new to his door.

Still, he wasn't tired of talking shop. The game was the fabric of the man, and he remembered the times, the innings, the pitches, the lineups, and the style of baseball he played for all those years. He talked with a heavy Southern accent, one that obscured names and places, but he spoke slowly, with that marvelous baseball ramble that strung sentences to infinity and effortlessly moved from one player to the next, one moment in history to another. Clarabelle tiptoed about the room, showing a fearful reverence for the tape recorder and occasionally placing her finger to her lips in a promise that she would not disturb the conversation.

Only moments into our talk, she returned hurriedly to the room and over to the windows. "Hey, hear them sirens? Sound mighty close, don't they?" she said.

The noise was close, and when Mrs. Bell separated the blinds, the whirling lights of fire engines reflected off the room's walls.

Bell and I went to the window and saw firemen run into a house directly across the street. There were no visible flames, but smoke poured from the second-floor windows and firemen on the sidewalk poked long poles through the glass. In seconds a burning mattress came hurtling out of one of the windows, and firemen on the street hosed it down and beat it with shovels.

"Oh, that's pathetic!" Clarabelle said. "Those poor little things over there. It's pitiful!"

"Yeah, it's bad," Cool Papa said. "See, we know those people. We give them money sometime. . . ."

A set of mattress springs came flying out of the same window.

"Those people have lost their home up there, Bell!" Clarabelle said. She shook her head from side to side, the lights of the fire trucks illuminating her face. "Ain't that pitiful! They stand up there, they don't have no home!"

Even before the fire, the Bells said they had tried to help the family out, even when one of the boys got into trouble with the police, yet nothing seemed to do any good. The fire was but another tribulation, and in the face of it, as minor as it appeared to be, Cool Papa and Clarabelle hung their heads, as if the blaze had hit their own home.

"We'll give them some money," Cool Papa said once again.

One by one the fire engines left, but it was difficult to turn the subject back to baseball.

Clarabelle paced the room. "I'll try not to say no more about it," she promised. "It's pathetic, as you saw yourself, but it's what we're going through."

"It really upsets us," said Cool Papa.

He went on about the neighborhood, about how kids stood in front of the grocery down the block and picked wallets and purses. Even he had to be careful just walking down the street. "I got to watch out all the time," he insisted. He said he was taking pills for hypertension and for the arthritis in his knee. Clarabelle, too, he said, was under a doctor's care for her nerves.

She returned to the blinds again. "We going to have to put up some money, Bell," she said.

He shook his head. "I never have made a whole lot of money, but somehow we give it out and some way we live."

That gave way to a discussion of how much money he made as a ballplayer.

"Ninety dollars a month starting out as a pro in St. Louis in 1922. Four hundred fifty as a Homestead Gray during World War Two." He followed with thoughts of salaries and contracts, and how the economics of Negro baseball were as much a daily concern to the players as the game itself.

The stories then began to pour from him, tales of Satchel, Josh, the good teams, the great teams, the rolling era of Negro baseball during Cool's thirty years in it. Many of his anecdotes and descriptions had a familiar ring to them. Bell by that time had made himself accessible to the modern baseball historians who were reexamining the sport, and he had always kept in touch with a good number of fellow players around the country; hence his recollections were passed on and reprinted through the years in a variety of places. The Trujillo encounter of 1937 was his favorite, included in almost every interview he had given. Earl Mack's $100,000 price tag on Cool's talents in 1934 was another.

Mrs. Bell finally went to the telephone to call her sister and report the fire; Cool Papa brought out his fat scrapbooks. They were filled mostly with newspaper accounts from black and Spanish-language papers of games he'd been in. There were also some fine black-and-white photos, many taken in the 1930s when he was with the Crawfords, some of them showing him in action: beating out a bunt, sliding safely into third base at Griffith Stadium. Many were posed team pictures, the ones so common among the black teams of the era: teams standing shoulder to shoulder along a baseline for a wide-angle shot taken at such a distance that the faces of the players are almost impossible to discern. Other photos showed Cool Papa with Satchel, Josh, playing around with Crutchfield and Sammy Bankhead.

Many of Cool's photos by that time were familiar to me, for as important as the scrapbook was to him, he never hesitated when asked permission to reprint photos from it. That generosity created problems for him. His new notoriety, he explained, had brought fan mail from all over. Much of it contained requests for autographs, pictures, information, souvenirs—almost anything people thought they wanted and felt like asking for. It troubled Bell because he was almost incapable of turning people down. He worried that he would be tricked or defrauded by someone using his signature on checks, credit cards, or legal documents. He was afraid people would attach it to phony wills or affidavits which would award them something which belonged to Bell and his family. Nothing of the sort had happened yet, but Bell had read of it and it fairly scared him.

He was not nearly so perturbed about ways in which he had already been shortchanged. Although he had permitted his photographs to be reprinted numerous times, he had never received any payment. He had sent a sheaf of photos off to *Look* magazine as part of a piece they were doing on the Negro leagues, and not only did he get no money in return, but he was unable to get his pictures back. It took months of letters and calls before the photos were finally returned to him.

He also felt wronged by newspaper and television reporters. One asked that he pose for a photo holding a cane, something he had used after a knee operation but had long since discarded. The photo, however, implied that he was enfeebled and needed a walking stick, a notion that insulted a man who still took pride in his legs and how well they served him.

Bell, however, wasn't resentful of such treatment; it simply made him more and more nervous about life in general. Talking about baseball, dealing with the possibility of being inducted into the Hall of Fame—that he could cope with. But life with clamoring fans, a tough neighborhood, his health and Clarabelle's—those things worried him. And then, occasionally, a house on the street would break into flames.

As it grew close to midnight, Clarabelle returned to the living room and paged through the scrapbooks. She joined in when Bell talked about the color ban which had kept him out of big-league baseball. Like most of the players of his generation, almost to a man, he refused to admit to any bitterness over the injustice.

"We had good white people, but they had to accept what the public accepts. They were good people, but they couldn't speak out for you because they would get hurt," he said.

"That's right," Clarabelle interjected. "That's the whole thing."

"Don't think all white people are bad like some people say. I'm a Christian and I don't believe that. People were afraid to speak out. A lot of white owners wanted to sign us, but they couldn't speak out," Cool said.

But neither of them really wanted to linger over the issue, the discrimination, the hatred in some places in the South, the urine thrown from the stands. That was all done and over with, and they were not now about to create a bad impression of themselves or black people in general by railing about it.

"That's me when I first married Bell. Wasn't I cute?" Clarabelle said. "That was taken in Havana, Cuba. See, big legs, little bitty thing . . ."

"I hit with my hands apart on the bat," Bell said, trying to get our attention on a picture of him across the page.

"That's me again when we were married," Clarabelle said. "Look how tiny I was."

She flipped more pages. "You ever heard of Louise Beavers, who played in *Imitation of Life?* She autographed this for me . . . Louise Beavers. She's dead now. . . ."

They both went silent, lost in the clippings and the memories, and the room, save only for the brush of pages, was quiet with them. Then Bell grabbed my elbow.

"There they are! Those five," he exclaimed. He tapped a now-famous 1932 photo of Rap Dixon, Josh, Judy Johnson, and Jud Wilson talking with Crawford player-manager Oscar Charleston. "I'd take those guys over anybody—Dixon, Gibson, Wilson, Johnson, and Charleston—them five right there. I'd take 'em over anyone!"

He pushed his glasses up, pinched what was left of a lemon peel, and shook his head. The photo lay there and lived for him. He whistled through his teeth. It was getting late, but he could have gone on for hours. He had an avid listener on his hands, his books were hot, and the times had come alive.

When I finally got up to leave, Bell went into the dining room to get his hat so he could see me out to my car.

"If you just get in and keep on going," he advised, "you'll be okay."

Nevertheless, he opened a desk drawer and pulled out a revolver and leather holster. It was the gun he used for work, he explained, and he had to have it around the house because of the neighborhood. A burglar had tried to come through a bedroom window only awhile ago, he said, and that terrified Clarabelle.

He held the holster in his left hand and put his right hand on the gun's handle, and we walked outside. It was cold and still; we could both see our breath and smell the remains of the charred mattress lying on the curb. Though it was dark, there seemed nothing on Dickson Street particularly foreboding, nothing meriting the pistol Cool Papa Bell cradled in his hands. But he held it in front of him, and I got into my car. He was standing there, those once-great legs, wrists, eyes that used to see the seams of a curveball, in front of his white picket fence, an old man with a hat on his head and a gun in his hand, and I drove off.

13

Crutch

I was to see Cool Papa again just over two years later. My first novel, *The Bingo Long Traveling All-Stars and Motor Kings* was published that summer, 1973, and summertime being to publishing what hot weather is to ambition, I looked for ways to create interest in the book. It was suggested by a friend that a luncheon be held to kick off its publication. His idea was to invite book review editors, sportswriters, and anyone else interested to sit over the meal and talk black baseball and *Bingo Long*. The center of attention, however, would be a few Negro league stars and their reminiscences. It was my chance to show Cool Papa my appreciation for the night of memories he had shared with me in St. Louis.

His life had not changed much in two years. He had retired from his watchman's job, and he now spent his nights with Clarabelle. Both of them still fought bad health, the hypertension and arthritis, and it had become a consuming topic with them. A casual "How are you, Cool Papa?" brought on a detailed recounting of problems and aches and medications. Still, none of his maladies was enough to keep Bell out of circulation. He answered his phone, returned letters with shaky, tortured handwriting, and went about his neighborhood on visits and errands. The invitation to come up to Chicago by train (he no longer drove and felt ill at ease on airplanes) was accepted and the date set.

Part of the attraction for Bell was a chance to see "Crutch,"

165

his old teammate Jimmie Crutchfield. The little right fielder from Moberly, Missouri, had settled in Chicago and worked for the post office until retirement. He then split his time between his apartment on Chicago's South Side and a summer home he and his wife owned in South Haven, Michigan. It wasn't easy to catch him in Chicago during the summer, but he readily accepted the luncheon invitation.

Just before the affair, I picked up Cool Papa from his hotel, and together we drove down Lake Shore Drive to the South Side and Crutchfield. We parked in a large lot in front of the building and headed for the entrance. Then Jimmie appeared, walking quickly out the front door, his face animated with a wide smile.

"Cool!" he yelled.

"Crutchfield!" Cool Papa replied, also breaking into a grin.

Jimmie held both his hands in front of him and excitedly shook Bell's; two skinny lightning-quick outfielders who'd backed each other up forty years before, now genuinely glad to be together once again, that Crawford style one more once.

Crutchfield lived on South Cottage Grove in an area near Thirty-fifth Street called Lake Meadows. Chicago is a city which covers such a wide area that residents of one side of town often know next to nothing about those of another. It is also a subtly segregated city, with sharply defined ethnic neighborhoods reminiscent of fifty years before, a characteristic which moved Norman Mailer to call it "the most American of American cities." The South Side, which contains the city's largest black population, is divided into black and white sections by certain main streets, some of them such definite boundaries that a black knows very well not to diagonally cross certain intersections. Years of civil rights progress have broken the barriers down some, but they still prevail.

On sheer geographic levels, it is not uncommon for blacks who live on the South Side to know nothing of blacks who live on the

West Side, or those in small pockets on the largely white North Side. (Chicago has no East Side, for the most part, because it borders Lake Michigan; only sections of the South Side of the city have east and west notations.) Conversely, whites living on the city's North Side seldom travel to the South or West sides, nor do they get to white sections on the far South or Southwest sides. This says nothing of the sprawling suburban areas whose residents often remark that they haven't been inside the city for years.

Such divisions do more than just make strangers of fellow Chicagoans. They also hinder any real perception of what life in other parts of the city is all about. Whites learn about ghetto living from the newspapers and generally associate tales of gangs, public housing, and random violence with all-black or Latin neighborhoods, Such generalizations make no allowance for areas like Thirty-fifth and Cottage Grove, and for the many households like the Crutchfields, which, while black, are as middle class as can be. Their neighborhood reflects their values as well as their problems: new shopping centers, attractive, well-maintained high-rise apartment buildings, and compact cars combine with barricaded storefronts and carry-out shops with armed guards. On bright summer afternoons, it is clean and bustling, with bug-eyed kids being led by well-dressed mothers and older sisters, while black businessmen and professionals, bus drivers, and postal clerks go about their day.

Crutchfield's apartment complex was one of a series in the neighborhood filled largely with middle-class blacks. His apartment was on the seventh floor, and he buzzed visitors up without concern. The elevators were clean and efficient, dull as they should be, not the stereotyped elevators in housing projects which are terrorized by gangs or simply seldom working. Again, as if to defy what too many whites believe about the way in which blacks live, the elevator just hummed and stopped at the seventh floor.

At sixty-five, with touches of gray at his temples, Jimmie was as short at five-foot-eight as ever. There was still an edge to him, a contained, punctuated way of carrying himself. He had been in the hospital for abdominal surgery, but he looked fit, healthy, and trim with his tight, radiant smile and a handshake. He introduced Julia, his wife of thirty-one years. She was a light-skinned woman wearing a gray wig, and she greeted me with a reserved, almost embarrassed manner. A bright, articulate woman, Mrs. Crutchfield taught school for many years, yet she became an opinionated ball fan like so many of the wives of Negro players. Their apartment was small, a single bedroom with tile floors and an assortment of chairs around a small color television set, an exercise bicycle in a corner. The most noticeable furnishings were the shelves of books, many with faded cloth jackets, and magazines—*The New Yorker, Ebony*—and stacks of worked-over Sunday papers.

Jimmie, dressed in a short-sleeved shirt and Bermuda shorts, sat down in an overstuffed red vinyl chair. Few former ballplayers were so articulate and thoughtful. He spoke slowly, phrasing his thoughts as if he knew he was going to be quoted. He had learned how to put words together so that people would remember them. He, too, had scrapbooks.

"I was so small when I started playing," he said, "that people constantly told me I was never going to make it. I figured I had to keep a scrapbook right from the beginning just to show them. There aren't but one or two players who have better books than mine."

Then his stories also rolled out—the golden years with the Crawfords; the 1935 All-Star game and his barehanded catch; Josh; the breakup of the Craws and the years with other teams. He had photos of a sensational head-on crash his Newark Eagle team bus had with a car on a highway in West Virginia. Had the bus not veered into a filling station next to the road, it would have gone down the side of a mountain and probably killed them all. Crutchfield laughed and shook his head at the photo showing the bus half inside the station.

The stories went on with each scrapbook page. The books were not kept in the apartment, Crutchfield said, but in his automobile. His smooth, snub-fingered fielder's glove was also there. His car had burglar alarms and was a safer place for the priceless souvenirs than his apartment, he believed, and less vulnerable to thieves and fire. He mentioned the one memento he held in a safe-deposit box. That was the autograph he got from Josh during the 1946 All-Star game. Jimmie had Satchel's on the same piece of paper, and he always considered it a treasure.

He talked of Josh like a brother, a person he spent a lot of time with, and thought a lot of. To Crutch, who was hard-pressed to come up to Josh's shoulders and weighed seventy-five pounds less, Josh was still a boy, a good-natured tender, callow boy.

"Josh was such a . . . a . . ."—and he hesitated for the right emphasis—"such a *nice* guy."

And in looking over Josh's career, with its amazing accomplishments, its heights, and its swift decline, Jimmie was moved to speak of the man's heart, of a soft psyche and spirit which were finally broken. And Jimmie, ever the feisty, independent, yet wise little man, knew well what he was talking about. He often looked silently off as he rekindled the memory of Josh's sparkling countenance and boyish soul.

Mrs. Crutchfield added her own impressions, the playful ways Josh talked, the accents he like to mimic. She explained that she wasn't as close to the ball teams as were some of the other wives. She was a schoolteacher, and her education set her apart from the others. "I always felt a certain estrangement, nothing definite, but it was there," she said. Still, she remembered the times when the wives, especially Satchel's wife, Janet, who was called "Toad" because of her big eyes, got together and prepared wonderful Southern-cooked meals of pig's feet, lima beans and corn bread. The meals brought the players and their wives together like no other times in the life of a fraternity which was broken by trades, schedules, wintertime, and so many other factors which naturally separated ball teams.

Jimmie could have gone on for hours about the old times, just as so many of the old stars can. But he didn't cleave to the scrapbooks or depend on the memories. He had put in twenty-five years with the post office in Chicago, then three years as a bank messenger, and he was proud of those years, too. He and his wife were mobile, modern, thoughtful people, and though they worried about the neighborhood and their safety ("There's just too much hatred around these days"), they were not depressed by it. Crutchfield worried instead about Cool Papa and Cool's health. The two of them talked often by phone, and Crutchfield had to calm Bell and try to persuade him not to worry about things. Jimmie, again the big little man, backing up a fellow outfielder, even after so many years.

"I get the books out once in a while. And I can tell people who say, 'I never heard of you,' a lot of things. I wasn't just a run-of-the-mill ballplayer. I contributed something.

"But I never get into that much anymore. It's too late now. It's all over and gone," he said.

And Crutch, the mite from Moberly, smiled in his gracious, mischievous way, the same way he had decades back when they told him he was just too small to make it.

14

Bankhead

For some of the other Crawfords, retirement and old age were neither gracious nor comfortable. Old ballplayers do die, over and over again, in ninth innings past and future. Somehow the last man is always retired, the field empties, and the shouting ends. Yet ballplayers like Sammy Bankhead kept hearing the echoes.

He would never be mentioned with the greats of the game, not the Gibsons, Paiges, Charlestons, and Bells, but he was a solid ballplayer, a versatile, fluid infielder, outfielder, and, later, a knowledgeable manager. Sammy Bankhead was the eldest of five Bankhead brothers—Dan, Fred, Joe, and Garrett were the others—born in Mississippi but raised in Empire, Alabama, where he learned his baseball. Sam first played for Southern League teams, Nashville and Birmingham, before coming north to Pittsburgh and the Crawfords.

There he met Helen, a girl from nearby Homestead who had grown up with Cum Posey's kids around West Field, where the Grays sometimes played. Later, she and her friends went to the Crawford Grille to meet the ballplayers. Sam was one of the quieter, more introspective players, good-looking, intelligent. Yet when teammate Jimmie Crutchfield introduced him to Helen, he opened up and spent long hours with her in the booths and in front of the long bar of the Grille. They were married in 1937 and began a partnership like that of all ballplayers and their wives: one constantly marked by separation and travel. Occasionally, winters were spent together in exotic places like Venezuela or San Juan, but most of the time, wives like Helen Bankhead remained alone back in Pittsburgh.

Now, forty years later, a portly, soft-spoken tired woman, Helen could look back and talk of how she had silently put up with the problems and the inconveniences. Back then, she followed the game and knew the players and the personalities and the intricacies of the profession. She passed along team gossip to other wives, was close to some and alienated from others. Sometimes she talked long hours to Dorothy Harris, Vic's wife, who usually knew what had gone on during this trip or that one. As the years passed, she coped with the agonies brought on by a part-time husband; somehow she remained close to Sammy and retained an affection for his tempered ways.

In 1939, the couple had a daughter named Brenda, and two years later a son, Anthony. By then Sam was playing with Josh and the Grays in summer, and going to Puerto Rico and South America in winter. He wasn't much of a father to his children, as Helen never really expected him to be. In her own reserved, methodical way, she got by and kept the household intact. It seemed as though Sammy would never get out of baseball, that he never wanted to, and, like so many of his teammates, saw nothing past the game and felt lost without it.

By the late 1940s he had become player-manager of the Grays. He was a dependable, natural leader, so much so that young players went to him for help and direction, especially young Josh Gibson, Jr. Sammy looked on Josh's boy as his own son, knowing his quiet personality just as well as he knew Josh's raucous, careless nature. He tried a little harder with Josh, Jr., because he knew how little Josh had given. Ironically, Sammy's own boy, Tony, who by then was still an adolescent, did not get the same amount of attention. Helen saw that, and she wondered and worried about it.

In 1950, after the Grays folded, Sammy was signed by the Pirates to manage their Farnham, Quebec, farm club, and in so doing, he became the first black manager in white organized baseball. It was an impressive, though uncelebrated milestone. And short-lived. While with Farnham, Sammy worked with Josh, Jr., until the boy broke his foot.

Sammy stayed on in Farnham until 1952, when the club asked him to take a cut in salary. It was finally something in baseball Sammy could not accept, and at the age of forty-two, he quit the game for good. He returned to Pittsburgh and went to work, not in baseball or sports promotion or something related to the game he had spent his life in, but on a city garbage crew. It was a steady, decent-paying job, one with the extra benefit of a foreman who was a longtime Pittsburgh ball fan. He had long admired Sammy and gave him choice assignments and easy shifts. Years passed with the crew, time no longer marked by plays or series or averages, weeks and months that merged until Sammy no longer really cared about how time went by or how fast.

He took up regular drinking with the garbage crew. They drank after work or on Saturday mornings, playing cards and talking times, usually old times, with Sammy babbling more as he became drunker. By then he had switched from beer to wine, as much of it as any man could drink. When he got loaded, Helen watched him go from a quiet, pensive man to a blabbermouth, a jabbering, self-appointed expert who thought he would settle all arguments and top all stories. He became estranged from his old teammates, seeing them less and less, seemingly not caring about the rift.

At the same time, his son, Tony, began to develop a passion for baseball, playing on sandlot teams and yearning desperately to make it to the pros. Sammy, however, refused to push him, or even direct him to any degree. "You're a father to so many boys," Helen would say, "but not to your own son." But it had little effect, and Tony went about trying to prove himself on his own. In his teens, he was scouted by the pros but never signed. Once when he missed a pro tryout session in Pittsburgh, he became so severely depressed about it that his mother considered professional help. Still, Sammy didn't pay much attention. While he would stop and fuss with neighborhood kids playing ball in the street, he let Anthony alone.

He also drank more, especially on Saturday mornings, and his drunks lasted longer. He drank on Fridays and Saturdays, then on Thursdays, too; and as the years passed, the drunk days of the week increased until he was sober only on Sunday. And Helen, resigning herself to the routine, would say that she couldn't wait for Sunday so she could have at least one day of peace, one day in which Bankhead wasn't jabbering in his cups.

Things with Anthony got worse, especially when the boy entered his twenties and knew all too well that his life's ambition of professional baseball was awash. He went off once with a barnstorming team headed by Satchel Paige, and Helen feared the worst because she was certain Tony couldn't cope with the rigors of a traveling team. She was right, for in less than two months she got word that Tony was stranded and destitute in Chicago. Among other problems, he had almost starved to death. He came back to Pittsburgh with his spirits crushed, his baseball ambitions extinguished, and a psyche totally unable to cope with itself.

Tony then began regular visits to Mayview State Hospital, a mental facility, but treatment there seemed to do little for his manic-depressive condition. He was only in his twenties, yet as he grew older his condition grew no better. Helen had no solutions; Sammy withdrew deeper into his own problems. Tony's stays at Mayview became longer, his reasons to leave the facility, at least in his own mind, almost nonexistent. In 1970 he became physically ill. Doctors diagnosed cancer of the colon. In a matter of months, Tony, at age twenty-nine, was dead. Sammy stopped drinking long enough to bury his son, then he went back to his daily binges with the crew.

Helen, by this time, after long years of living with a man in love with the bottle, had resigned herself to the situation and lived her life in spite of it. She developed a stoic, almost placid demeanor. "They get drunk every day," she would say to her friends. "Ballplayers or not. Show me one who doesn't."

In 1972, Sammy had twenty years in with the city, and he retired. But he and Helen soon learned that he was to receive no pension because when he'd started the job, he had failed to join the credit union. The family protested and complained and petitioned everyone involved, but the answer was always the same: Sam was entitled to Social Security and nothing more. They were living in a sparsely furnished apartment above a dry-cleaning store on Wylie Avenue in the Hill District, and the fruits of Social Security weren't enough to change that.

As a retiree, Sam stayed around the apartment and read— when he was sober and when he was drunk. He read newspapers, magazines, and what few books he could lay his hands on, he read two and three times. Then he drank some more, usually walking slowly up Wylie Avenue to a tavern where he played cards and filled up. He insisted that drinking was the only thing that gave him any pleasure in life, and he was going to do it. He no longer stayed sober even on Sundays. When drunk with his buddies, he continued as self-appointed arbiter, starting and ending arguments, lording his knowledge acquired from his reading over fellow lushes who read nothing at all.

He stayed away from the ball park, however, no matter what the occasion or how strong the invitation. Although he never said it in so many words, watching major-league baseball was somehow painful for him, an experience he couldn't bear. He feigned disinterest and left it at that, but it was an antipathy so deeply ingrained that one time, after securing a section of free tickets to a Pirate game for himself and some friends, he left after the first inning and went home. Helen was dumbfounded and asked him why, but Sammy just shook his head, paused, then went off alone.

He didn't show the same reticence when it came to talking about the game, especially the old days, the old games, topics incessantly rehashed. Gray-Crawford games were replayed *ad nauseam*. Still Sammy avoided any contact with his old teammates. He had nothing to do with Ted Page or Sam Streeter, both of whom lived in Pittsburgh, and when people like Chet Brewer passed through town, Sammy wouldn't even return their phone calls. He didn't go to any of the reunions or the banquets, and he steadfastly refused to go to Cooperstown, New York, to witness Hall of Fame proceedings.

"Why? What would I do while they're going through all that?" he would protest to Helen.

"You'd sit there and act like a gentleman, that's what," she would reply, but to no avail.

And finally the invitations stopped coming, and his old friends wrote him off.

Each morning he would slowly wind his way up Wylie Avenue to his saloon and his cards, and later on he would stumble back. He made no apologies, and with the same sly sense of things that had made him the effective ballplayer and manager that he had been, he knew when the people on the street watched him and shook their heads. They were the same ones who commiserated with Helen and asked her how she survived, and to whom she would say, "They all get drunk every day; show me one that doesn't."

One day she spotted him coming down Wylie Avenue, and she cocked her head in wonderment as she watched him walk a zig-zag pattern down the street for blocks until he got to the house.

"What was that all about, Bankhead?" she said, realizing that he wasn't at all tipsy.

"Ladies on the street all lookin' for me to stumble like a drunk," he said. "I wasn't gonna let 'em down." And he went inside to his magazines.

But retirement slowly began to grate on him, and in late 1975 he decided to get a job just for something to do, something to keep him in drinking money. So many guys retired from the garbage crew, he said, then went home and died. He wasn't

ready for that. He signed on as a dishwasher at the William
Penn Hotel in downtown Pittsburgh. Soon he became well-liked
there, for he managed to hold down his drinking on the job and
reveal his old gentle, efficient personality. He was quiet and
courteous to the women who worked in the kitchen, and often
helped them with heavy pans and pots and trays. His daily
routine consisted of walking up the hill in the morning to drink
and play cards, then hopping a bus for the job around 2:00 P.M.
and working from 3:00 to 10:30, and finally knocking off for a
bottle and a bull session before taking the midnight bus back
home.

It went that way into 1976, the year he lost two brothers:
Dan, the one Bankhead who made it into the majors, as a
pitcher for Brooklyn for three seasons, who died in May of
throat cancer; and Fred, an infielder for the Memphis Red Sox
for many years, who died in an auto accident on his way to visit
the boys' mother.

Then came the night of July 24. Work was light at the hotel
that Saturday night, so Sammy and fellow employee Nelson
Cooper, a man in his seventies, knocked off early. In the
employee locker room they began arguing about who did the
most work. Cooper later claimed that Sammy slapped him twice,
and after the second time he told Sammy that if he did it again,
he'd kill him. Sammy slapped him once more, Cooper said,
before he went to his locker and got a small handgun. The two
men struggled. A hotel banquet steward saw them and hurried
after a security guard. When he returned, Sammy was slumped
on the floor, a bullet in his head.

Cooper said the gun went off as they struggled, that he had no
intention of shooting Sammy. "He was drunk as a dog. I never
seen him that drunk. He didn't know what he was doing,"
Cooper said. He pleaded guilty to murder but claimed self-
defense.

Helen Bankhead, mindful of all the drunken squabbles her
husband had gotten into over the years, had her doubts. Sammy

was a solidly built man, and she was certain that if there had been a struggle Sammy would have come out on top. From the giant bruise she said she saw on the back of Sammy's skull as he lay in the morgue, she was certain that he was first cold-cocked from behind, then shot. She waited only to learn the fate of Sammy's killer.

She watched with her two daughters and her grandchildren as he was buried on a sunny, hot July day. Among the pallbearers was Josh Gibson, Jr., unable to contain his grief for one who had treated him like a son. Yet Helen remained stolid and dry-eyed, with a calmness honed by so many tough years with "Bankhead."

Then she retired to the bare walls and the television set of her apartment above the dry cleaners on Wylie Avenue, and she went about what she was doing before the man she had lived with for thirty-eight years was shot in the head. She was a survivor, and she would continue to survive.

Then she looked about her, sighed, and said almost inaudibly, "So, that's that."

15

Ballplayers First

They tried to get together every year or so. It hadn't always been like that, but as the time passed, as the memory and the camaraderie of the Negro leagues began to fade, the former players and their wives decided that they should make the effort and not let such a unique, significant past die.

One of the movers was Ted Page. He made use of an association with the Gulf Oil Company to arrange a reunion in June 1972 in a suite at Chicago's Sherman House Hotel. Seventeen veterans of various teams and leagues, most living in the Midwest, showed up for dinner and stories, then posed for a photo session with newsmen from Chicago's black press. It was a low-key, sentimental evening—with the necessary publicity for Gulf Oil—and those who gathered—Crutchfield, Bell, Alex and Ted Radcliffe, David Malarcher, and Jack Marshall, among others—savored the fact that they were still alive and lucid and able to look back.

But changes in the public-relations policy at Gulf kept Page from repeating the fete, and in coming years the task of raising money and organizing the get-together was left to the players themselves. It was not easy, for funds were meager, and so many ballplayers were ailing, or getting too old to get around anymore, or had passed away. But in June 1975, another "old-timers" dinner was set, again in Chicago, this time ostensibly to honor Cool Papa Bell and his recent induction into the Hall of Fame. Facilities were reserved at the Stockyard Inn, a restaurant and motel which once served a bustling cattle and meat-packing industry in the acres of pens surrounding it. Just south was Chicago's International Amphitheater, the huge hall which hosted the 1968 Democratic National Convention, among many others, and which still welcomed circuses and professional wrestlers and flea markets. By the 1960s, the meat-packing industry had become segmented and localized, and the stockyards of Chicago were deserted. No longer did cattle owners, haulers, packers, butchers, and cowboys stay over at the inn, eating their own prime cuts and drinking too much liquor. By the time the old-timers sought to rent the inn for their reunion, it gladly accommodated them, for business was scarce.

They scheduled what they called a press conference in the afternoon preceding the night's banquet. They gathered in a rear reception room in the inn, an area one got to after walking through dusty corridors no doubt elegant forty years earlier when the suites were full, but which in 1975 were gray and drab and decrepit. The meeting room, however, was comfortable and stately, decorated with tremendous portraits of Irish meat-packing barons. It may have been a little to appropriate that a room which once had oozed aristocracy and expensive liquor should that day be filled with the great-grandchildren of slaves, all dressed in sport coats and ties, white shoes and dress shirts, talking about the old days when they were delivered from working as porters or mail carriers by playing baseball in a segregated league in a segregated country.

Jack "Boisy" Marshall, once a tough second baseman for the Chicago American Giants, was one of the prime organizers of the reunion, and he moved about in a suit but no tie. He looked better than he did from day to day when he wore a nylon windbreaker in the dusty backroom of his bowlers' supply shop on Chicago's South Side. He was missing front teeth, and that was evident when he moderated the press conference. Yet as hard as Boisy tried, there is no such thing as a late Saturday afternoon press conference in the middle of the summer for men who made news forty years ago. No reporters from the major Chicago dailies were there; only a few writers from black papers and one photographer had made the trip.

The gathering was really a sophisticated bull session. Cool Papa was the center of attraction, dressed in his red plaid sports coat, his knees rising high off the floor as he sat. He was looking good but feeling awful, again complaining about his health.

"The doctor told me I was taking my life into my hands by coming up here," he said. "But I said that I am a ballplayer first. Three days ago, I didn't know if I was going to make it. . . ."

He rambled on, as he had the first night I met him, an endless, Casey Stengel-type talker, stories that went into each other and seemed never to end.

He was interrupted occasionally by David Malarcher, the spry, stately old man of Chicago baseball who, at eighty-one, had as much fire in his eyes as anyone. Malarcher had a high, lilting voice, and nobody could remember when Chicago Negro league baseball hadn't included him, first as a third baseman, then as a crafty, persuasive manager. "Gentleman Dave," as he was known, told a better story than anyone.

He went on about Rube Foster, Bingo DeMoss, Chet Brewer, always prefacing each tale with a superlative ("the greatest manager who ever lived"; "the finest second baseman I ever saw") and then began his story of Cool Papa. He was marveling at Bell one game, he said, because everything the American Giants hit into the outfield Bell speared. "Then one of my batters hit one that was a sure home run, and I yelled, 'Okay, Cool, try and get that one!' And Cool took off with such swiftness that I quickly added, 'I didn't mean it! I didn't mean it!!' "

And Malarcher rocked in his chair as he laughed, and the others around him laughed and nodded their heads at Cool Papa.

Ted Page was also there, the only one to come from as far

away as Pittsburgh, one of the few to arrive at the inn with his wife via a taxi. In a summer suit and matching shoes, Page reflected the comfortable living he'd made as a bowling alley proprietor and community worker since his baseball days. When Page spoke, he quickly became sentimental, finally philosophizing not about baseball or Cool Papa but about life and growing old. He told about how Jack Marshall had given him a job in a bowling alley just after his playing days were over. How just recently his auto had broken down on the highway and some people had unselfishly come to his aid. He went on about having friends, the virtue of staying close, of helping people, and his listeners silently, knowingly nodded their graying heads.

The afternoon drifted on; more players appeared; some left. George "Jew Baby" Bennett, an outfielder for a half dozen Negro teams, whose white skin made obvious the origin of his nickname, sat in a corner and said nothing. Wearing plaid pants and a striped sport coat, Bennett finally got up and hurried around the room asking everyone, even reporters and the photographer, to sign his autograph book. Normal "Tweed" Webb, a former utility infielder who since his playing days had made a profession of organizing and chronicling baseball, followed close behind Bennett. Perhaps no man in the country was a more dedicated historian of Negro baseball than Tweed Webb. With a neon smile, Tweed handed out mimeographed sheets of statistics he'd compiled, or copies of newspaper clippings, or publicity he'd generated in his unceasing effort to get more blacks into the Hall of Fame. "I don't know the answer right off," he'd reply to questioners, "but I'll try to research it and send it to you."

Finally, the group broke up into small clusters, some looking at Tweed Webb's data, others standing shoulder to shoulder for rigidly smiled photos. Ted Page made a point of showing an action photo of Cool Papa legging out a bunt. "See, he's already past first base and the pitcher's just picked up the ball," Page said. "Proves how fast he was." Jack Marshall was asked if a couple of well-known old-timers would be there, and he answered that they never showed up when they had to pay for it. A large plate of corned beef and rye bread was set out as a snack with cocktails. Most of the players ignored it, but as the room began to fill with cocktail guests, a few newcomers began to dig in. Ted Page went over for a bite and was elbowed out of the way by a rotund gentleman who heaped the beef on a slice of bread, doused it with horseradish, and stuffed it into his mouth with such force that Page looked at him sideways and said, "You sure are greedy, ain't you, man." The stranger mumbled something, chewed loudly, and ambled away.

Jack Marshall finally brought the preliminaries to an end, but not before Ted Page added in closing, "And I'm *older* than Satchel Paige." It was seemingly unrelated to the general discussion, but it drew a marked response. Satchel was not there and was not expected. He seldom showed up at such gatherings. As a player he had always kept himself aloof from his teammates, preferring to make his own deals and meet his own timetables. He made few close friends, something which didn't change when he retired. His entire life in baseball had been pretty much focused on Satchel Paige; the other players knew it then, they'd known it ever since, and to some measure they resented it. That Satchel would attempt to get mileage out of the fact the he claimed he didn't know how old he was—a gimmick sportswriters doted on—was kind of a tedious game to black men such as these who knew the vagaries of coming from broken, intransigent families, and of having no birth certificates. They knew how old Satchel was, and he knew it. They also knew how good he was, and they would not begrudge him that. But they were also well aware of how good everybody else was, and the common struggles endured.

The afternoon fading, Cool Papa got up and announced to everyone that because of his health he had to pass up the cocktail hour. "I can't stand to be in crowds, as I get nervous and begin to break out in a rash," he said, and moved only when Jimmie Crutchfield, his chauffeur for the day, appeared. Crutch was trim and relaxed in his tennis hat and Bermuda shorts, promising everyone there that he would see them later on when he returned with Bell for the dinner and the ceremonies. The two of them left while they could, before the ladies in long dresses and sparkling purses began to fill the reception areas and bring on the heat and the proximity that would cause Cool's nerves to bristle.

Compare them to any group of men from varied backgrounds who for a short period of time were thrown together in one place and you find few differences, except that in this case all of those involved were black and, once separated from the experience that bound them, they went back to the quiet, ordinary lives of black men. Few of them had any money or, apart from baseball, any skills or education. When their playing days were over, most of them took menial jobs—as bartenders, custodians, guards, postal workers, factory workers. A few went into business for themselves—in a bowling alley, a sports shop. Some of the more prosperous sold insurance or real estate.

Occasionally they would be discovered by younger friends, neighbors, maybe an inquisitive local sportswriter. But the burden of proof was always on them, for so often the questions came from people too young to have known black baseball, and greats like Josh, Paige, or Bell, and the former stars had to produce scrapbooks and clippings to authenticate who they were and what they had done.

Only Satchel attempted to live off his famous name. He pitched for the Indians and the Browns in the 1950s, long after his stuff was gone. Then he drifted in and out of baseball, on minor-league teams as a coach or a player, or on throwbacks to the black leagues: barnstorming clubs like the Kansas City Monarchs and the Indianapolis Clowns. With them he made token appearances, sometimes pitching to a few batters, bringing back memories for older fans who remembered him in his prime. In 1965, he was put under contract with the Kansas City A's so that he might qualify for a major-league pension. Three years later, he coached for the Atlanta Braves.

But even Satchel found more lean periods as a retiree than he'd have thought possible. Back in Kansas City where he lived with his wife and kids, he occasionally worked as a deputy sheriff. He got a part in a Western movie. Once he ran unsuccessfully for state office. Other times he worried about finding another gig, or just keeping the kids fed. When author William Price Fox visited him in 1965, Satchel was out of work and out of money. He gladly accepted a loan to get his car out of hock, and rewarded Fox with a meandering interview in which he emptied a fifth of whiskey and jawed long into the night.

When organized baseball finally opened its eyes to the Negro league ballplayers and what they had done, Satchel was the first person they looked to. In 1969, the Baseball Writers Association decided the Hall of Fame in Cooperstown had been segregated long enough. A separate section for Negro league stars was introduced, and after controversy over whether or not the exclusion of Negro league blacks from the general museum was indeed a continuation of the Jim Crow mentality that had barred them from organized baseball in the first place, it was decided that worthy Negro league stars would be inducted on their merits, alongside every other Hall of Famer. Satchel ·was the first inductee, and the ensuing publicity assured him once again of more lucrative popularity. He spoke at dinners and conventions, made television appearances and endorsements, and again went to work for a minor-league club. He remained the Satchel of old: aloof, undependable, demanding—he often asked up-front for a lump sum for interviews—yet was as vivacious, witty, and spontaneous as ever. The name had not lost its excitement, and he knew it.

Most of the famous Crawfords followed him into the Hall of Fame: Gibson, Bell, Judy Johnson, the late Oscar Charleston. (Charleston's induction was roundly approved by former players, for they dearly loved the way he had played the game. Many regarded him as the best all-around performer, the most perfect daily ballplayer in the history of Negro leagues. His sister went to Cooperstown to accept the honor.) They did it with grace and humility, traveling with family and friends to the sultry midsummer proceedings, and the Cooperstown audiences couldn't help but be touched.

To a man, they said it was their greatest honor. In spite of all the years, all the frustrations, this last tribute, they said, meant a hell of a lot. They were ballplayers first, as Cool Papa had said, and finally in the Hall.

Judy Johnson, the skinny third baseman for so many great Negro teams and later a scout for the Philadelphia Phillies, typified their gratitude. Judy couldn't contain his emotion as he made his acceptance speech at Cooperstown in 1975. He broke into tears, and his son-in-law, Billy Bruton, a former Milwaukee Brave and Detroit Tiger center fielder, came out of the audience to console him. After a few moments, Judy returned to the microphone and finished his speech. His final words: "I am so grateful!"

16

A Gravestone

The Gibsons—Josh, Jr., and his family and Josh's sister, Annie, went to Cooperstown in August 1972. They modestly accepted a posthumous tribute to Josh. Josh, Jr., called the recognition of his father a "beautiful thing."

Then they returned to Pittsburgh, where life remained hard and unromantic. Health problems continued to plague the family. In the late 1960s, Josh, Jr., had suffered from kidney failure, and only a massive drive within the Pittsburgh black community to raise $15,000 for use of a dialysis machine kept him alive until a kidney transplant was performed. Now he suffered from hypertension, as did Annie Mahaffey, but medication and proper medical care kept the malady under control, and the two of them went about their normal routines.

Although Josh had been given his proper place in the Hall of Fame, the family did not benefit economically, as many writers and researchers eager to find out about the famous catcher discovered. They made their way to the Mahaffey home on Charles Street on the North Side, a section of town the cabbies told them to stay away from. It was called Pleasant Valley, but it was little more than a decrepit black ghetto of winding streets which climbed up the hills surrounding the Allegheny River. The houses were ramshackle frames, most built right up to the sidewalks with no room left for grass or trees, no green save for an occasional stink vine climbing a utility pole. Kids ran in front of the houses or slithered down the gangways, and old blacks sat on the sidewalks in ragged overstuffed chairs. House numbers were painted freehand on the brick or the front door, in white or red paint. There was no illusion of prosperity or charm, few stores apart from a couple of taverns, and almost nowhere to get change for a ten-dollar bill to pay a cabbie.

At first, Annie talked to anyone who made the trip. She'd usher them into a front living room with plastic-covered and darkened windows, or down a long hallway to the kitchen, where likely as not a televison and radio played simultaneously. Annie looked remarkably like her brother. She was heavyset, with dark skin and a round, glistening face—*that* face, *those* features which black sports fans saw in their newspapers for years.

She spoke with a bit of a Southern accent and broke out of her matter-of-fact delivery only when recounting some of the jokes or high times Josh had shared with the family. She easily remembered her childhood, the family in Georgia, and those first years in Pittsburgh. She talked with authority about her brother when he was still her brother, the young, eager kid who went all over the city looking for a ball game. Later on, her brother became Josh Gibson, the superstar who was known all over the country, and he spent precious little time at home. Annie lived his life then only to the extent that he told her about it. She was a part of the family and a part-time parent to Josh's children, but his life was an exclusive one, and Annie was seldom much but a spectator to it. She remembered well, however, his last few years, especially because he then spent more time back home in Pittsburgh. And she related her story of his death. Occasionally Josh, Jr., or his twin sister, Mrs. Helen Dixon, came over to add their memories. But any visitor was struck by the fact that there were no mementos of Josh around, no scrapbooks, little of the memorabilia and souvenirs baseball players are known to collect. The family, by and large, lived its own life, in the present, not the past.

Upon the full rediscovery of the Negro leagues, the publication of histories, and wider recognition of the old stars, the Gibson family began to feel a certain amount of resentment about it all. There was a sense of once again being excluded from proper recognition, or what monies might be involved. Annie and her husband, Elmer, became embittered, and the welcome to those wanting to know about Josh was withdrawn. They developed hard feelings toward those former players who'd been photographed and quoted about Josh, who'd played with him and felt qualified to talk about his life and his personality. To the family, such events were another part of the manner in which they were prevented from getting that which they believed was theirs by virtue of their kinship with Josh Gibson, even though they did not know what they should have been getting, or how, or from whom.

To some, his death contained an element of martyrdom. Ted Page and Jimmy Crutchfield, both sincere, genuine men who ate and played and slept with Josh, have said more than once that they believe he died of a broken heart. And nobody doubts them, for Josh's presumed disappointment over not making the majors is a romantic, tragic notion that befits an athlete of such magnificence dying so young. Yet Josh was hardly a martyr. Throughout most of his career he was an example of pure discrimination in the world of athletics. He was a symbol of injustice, an example for anyone to see of Jim Crowism at its most blatant, but not a martyr.

Nor was he a pioneer, a radical, or a rebel. Josh did not take chances to better the plight of his race or his personal condition. He was not an outspoken, gutsy radical Paul Robeson, or a sanguine, defiant rebel like Jack Johnson. Josh was not a Jackie Robinson or, in fact, even a Satchel Paige, who often refused to play in towns where he couldn't eat or sleep. Josh never took such a stand. He remained a symbol of excellence to black people, but his fans never lived and died with the travails of his career as they did with those of Johnson, Robeson, and Robinson, or with Jesse Owens and Joe Louis. Blacks mostly shook their heads in dismay and frustration when they spoke of Josh Gibson: a talent denied, a victim of the times.

There is every indication that Josh would have coped badly with retirement from baseball. His health notwithstanding, he was coping badly with his fading years. There was much in his character similar to that of Sammy Bankhead. For Sammy, the absence of baseball never set well. As Helen Bankhead wistfully said of Sammy and his former teammates, "When they weren't playin', they were cryin'. When they *were* playin', they were cryin'."

Josh's death was a combination of disease and disillusionment, a simple, depressed, sick man no longer able to fight. He had already started to drink heavily, and at an earlier age than Bankhead. The urge came not from bitterness or the pain of not seeing the major leagues, but from the pain of several crippling diseases and of seeing a future devoid of an ability to get by in baseball or enjoy a living that the game had always brought him.

To encounter Jimmie Crutchfield, Cool Papa Bell, Judy Johnson, Ted Page, and so many other vintage stars of the Negro leagues is to encounter the survivors, the serene, beautiful men who have persevered. Josh had a lot of that in him when he was young and healthy, and he lost it when he aged and became ill. His death, though tragic, was not that of a fighter but of a victim.

So many people prefer to remember him only as that, and do not put him under the same scrutiny as Joe Louis, Paul Robeson, Jesse Owens, Jack Johnson, and other black athletes and personalities who fought the racial fight. It is easier to remember Josh as the talent that he was, especially easier for former teammates who wish to avoid hurting or degrading anyone, to talk baseball instead of racial identity. Baseball, while always being recognized as a part of the American tradition, actually has always been a contradiction of it. It has been a game and an institution ruled by tradition, changed not by violence or revolution as has been the case with so many racial matters in America, but by plodding members of the game's aristocracy. Despite the acute social crime that the color bar in baseball was—and the fact that it had been broken years earlier in boxing and football, among other sports—baseball limped along, a national pastime of bigotry. And most fans, though outraged, were unwilling to stop everything and to force the game to confront the issue or cease operation. Buck Leonard described it so well years later:

We played at Griffith Stadium one Sunday and a group was there and they came into the clubhouse and said they wanted to talk. "So all right go ahead and talk." They said, "Don't you fellas think you could play in the major leagues?" "Yeah, we think so." "Would you fellas like to play in the major leagues?" "Yeah, we'd like to play in the major leagues." "So then why don't ya protest or demonstrate?" And we said, "You fellas demonstrate and protest, we're gonna play. We don't have time to protest. We got to play the ball game." "Aren't you all part of the movement?" "We're part of the game, not the movement that you're advocating. We're not part of that. We're part of baseball."

And in being part of the game, of baseball, they became victims of it, tragically as in Josh's case, sadly as in the case of Leonard and the others. "We just loved to play the game," they said, and would say it over and over again through the years.

For Josh, it would be a fitting epitaph.

From time to time, the old-timers will come to Pittsburgh, or just pass through, and they'll linger and talk about what a great baseball town it used to be. They'll talk about the Grays and the smoky town of Homestead, about Cum Posey; then they'll mention Gus Greenlee, "Big Red," in his suspenders and white shirt, the Crawford Grille, Greenlee Field, and those exhilarating, momentous games between the Grays and the Craws. If they have time, they'll wind their way through the North Side or up in the Hill District, and they'll see that things there haven't changed much. People will tell them that those are mean neighborhoods now, but they will reply that you always had to watch your step there, always.

Inevitably, the talk will drift to Josh, and the old-timers will hold their heads in retelling the drives, the size of the man, the way he held the club and slaughtered things thrown at him. Again, those amazing shots will come to mind, the way the home runs of Josh Gibson soared and disappeared. And everyone present will feel a part of the man, his times, and the marvelous way he played the game.

In July 1975, Pedro "Pete" Zorilla came up from Puerto Rico for the major-league All-Star game being played at the city's Three Rivers Stadium. Zorilla had long promoted baseball in San Juan, at one time owning the Santurce club, during the years when it was the haven for winter players, particularly black ones. He was most interested when he got to Pittsburgh in looking up those close to Josh, his baseball idol and an unequaled star for many Puerto Ricans. To do it, he contacted Ted Page and suggested that he and Page make their way to the Allegheny Cemetery and Josh's grave.

Page knew the general area of the grave, but when he and Zorilla got in the vicinity, they couldn't find it. The ground was dotted with small round metal caps, most of them overgrown with grass. Page and Zorilla scratched around for some time, but finally realized that they were dealing with numbered grave markers, none of which would pinpoint Josh's grave unless Page could remember the exact spot or cap number. It was painfully obvious that the great Josh Gibson had lain for close to thirty years in an unmarked grave, and that even if anyone had been as curious about him as Page and Zorilla were, they never could have found it.

Page and Zorilla went back to town and looked up John Crunkleton, the longtime undertaker on the North Side who'd handled Josh's funeral. Crunkleton found the records which contained the plot and the grave number, and with them, Page and Zorilla went back to the cemetery. Finally they located Josh's grave.

Page then decided that something should be done about the grave's anonymity, and made it known that he was starting a fund drive for a proper stone. One of his first donors was Pirate first baseman Willie Stargell, for Stargell, the massive slugger who impatiently whirled the bat in jerky, slashing circles prior to a pitcher's delivery, who had nailed drives in stadiums all over the league as viciously as Josh once had done, had strong feelings about his roots. He gave Page $100 to start, and promised more if it was needed.

But Stargell's money and the other generous donations which immediately came to Page weren't needed. Once the office of the commissioner of baseball found out about the drive, it told Page that it would cover the cost of a suitable gravestone and all related expenses. It was a small matter for Page to follow through, and in a matter of weeks a stone with the proper data, declaring that the deceased was a famous Negro league ball-player for the Crawfords and the Homestead Grays, was placed over the grave. It was a simple, unassuming marker, but quite sufficient. For those who came to stand over it would bring their own information, their own stories and legends, their own regard for a man who loved to play the game and played it so unforgettably, that man named Josh.

Index

Aaron, Henry, 39, 139
Abbott, Robert C., 57-58
"African Dodger" game, 5
Ahern, Jimmie, 84
Alexander, Grover Cleveland, 33
Allen, Newt, 37
All-Star teams and games:
  East-West Negro League, 90-95, 100,
    108, 109, 115, 119, 123, 131, 141,
    143, 151, 168
  major-league, 31, 76-78
  in Negro leagues, 37-38, 51, 76-78, 90-
    95
American Giants, 10, 47, 48, 50, 69, 86
American League, 151
American Negro League, 10
Ammon Field, 11, 13, 59
"Amos 'n' Andy," 56-57
Amsterdam News, 148
Anson, Cap, 31, 34
Armstrong, Louis, 12
Atlanta Braves, 185
Austin, Frank, 141

Baltimore Black Sox, 27
Baltimore Elite Giants, 53, 140, 156
Baltimore Orioles, 58
Bankhead, Anthony "Tony," 172-174
Bankhead, Brenda, 172
Bankhead, Dan, 171, 177
Bankhead, Fred, 171, 177
Bankhead, Garrett, 171
Bankhead, Helen, 126, 128, 135-136,
  171-178, 190
Bankhead, Joe, 171
Bankhead, Sammy, 51, 68, 77, 90-91,
  106, 110, 116, 120, 126, 128, 130-
  131, 133, 134-135, 137, 144, 148,
  151-152, 154, 162
  after baseball career, 171-178
Banks, Ernie, 41, 155-156, 157
baseball, skills needed in, 19-20

Baseball's Hall of Fame, 159, 163, 179,
  182, 185-186, 187
Baseball Writers Association, 185
Bassett, Pepper, 101, 103-104, 109
Beale, Harry, 11
Beckworth, John, 46
Bell, Clarabelle, 15, 158-161, 163-164,
  165
Bell, James "Cool Papa," 2, 3, 32, 37, 45,
  50, 70, 72, 80, 86, 97, 101, 104, 106-
  109, 111, 116-117, 120, 124, 138,
  141, 148, 151
  in All-Star games, 91-94
  after playing career, 154-164, 165-166,
  170, 179-184, 185-186, 190
Bell, William, 86
Benjamin, Jerry, 141
Bennett, George "Jew Baby," 17, 182
Benson, Bullet Ben, 89
Benswanger, William, 117, 132
Beverly, Charles, 38
*Bingo Long Traveling All-Stars and
  Motor Kings, The,* 165
Birmingham Black Barons, 131, 134
black newspapers, 4, 12, 56, 57-58, 117
  sportswriters of, 26-27, 29-30, 82, 87,
  109
black players (*see also* Negro leagues):
  barred from major leagues, 57-58, 71-
    72, 100, 111, 138-139
  batting stride of, 40-42
  camaraderie of, 67-68, 179
  disciplining and umpiring of, 83-85
  in Latin America, *see* Latin America
  major-league entry of, 140-142, 151
  in majors, scrutiny of, 143-144
  in 1950s, 152-153
  racial politics and, 34-35, 137-138
  reminiscences of, 154-184
  salaries and contracts of, 61, 66, 83, 96,
    97, 99-110, 116-117, 119-124, 139-
    140

194

200